the skillet

COOKBOOK

A Street Food Manifesto

JOSH HENDERSON
Photographs by Sarah Jurado

SASQUATCH BOOKS
SEATTLE

Printed in the United States of America

Published by Sasquatch Books
17 16 15 14 13 12   9 8 7 6 5 4 3 2 1

Cover and interior photographs: Sarah Jurado
Cover and interior design and composition: Anna Goldstein

Library of Congress Cataloging-in-Publication Data is available.

ISBN-13: 978-1-57061-732-4
ISBN-10: 1-57061-732-5

Sasquatch Books
1904 Third Avenue, Suite 710
Seattle, WA 98101
(206) 467-4300
www.sasquatchbooks.com
custserv@sasquatchbooks.com

Certified Chain of Custody
SUSTAINABLE Promoting Sustainable Forestry
FORESTRY
INITIATIVE www.sfiprogram.org
SFI-01268

SFI label applies to the text stock

Contents

Huck, Kelli, and Wallace in her belly

To my wife, Kelli

The Skillet Story

This is the story of how I took my passion to the streets and anchored my roots in the seasons of the city.

In 2007 I bought an Airstream trailer for five grand and turned it into a street-food truck. I wanted to create modern American comfort food, sourced locally and made with skill. I served close to forty thousand people on the streets of Seattle that first year.

Street food is instant gratification parked on a city grid. It's noon; you're at your downtown office desk, starving. Maybe you forgot to eat breakfast. Maybe you can't do one more day of turkey and cheese sandwiches. My job is to satisfy a very simple need: hunger. But just as food nourishes, it also gathers. Street food is about community as well, about spreading a story through putting food in the hands of people. What I do is provide a convenience, a way of satisfying in real time.

I love the idea of underpromising and overdelivering. I am used to cooking on wheels, making whole feasts with only a Bunsen burner and a single frying pan. For about three years, I was a chef on commercial photo shoots. I'd pack all of my own cooking equipment in bins, load up an RV, and cook in Moab, Bend, Miami. It was the quintessential nomadic bachelor lifestyle. I'd wake up on a tarmac and serve a bunch of people eggs Benedict at 6 a.m. Good food doesn't require a giant kitchen and state-of-the-art equipment. It just requires the desire to make it happen anywhere and anytime.

Skillet really started back in 2006. After decades of cooking, I was working at a desk for a restaurant equipment manufacturer. Bored and browsing the Internet, longing to return to cooking, I became increasingly interested in street food. Over time, during my tenure at the Culinary Institute of America and cooking around the country, I'd discovered that most industries have three tiers: the people who do the crappy version, the middle-of-the-road folks, and the top-tier folks who do it the best. Street food had the first two categories down pat—but no one had yet attempted to put couture cuisine on wheels. I felt there was a niche there for us to fill. (Unfortunately, the city of Seattle didn't always agree, but more on that later.)

Street food shouldn't just be tacos. I originally thought about doing a grill cart, but the city's archaic laws at the time deemed them illegal. I realized I needed a full kitchen for the sort of meals I had in mind and started looking for different kinds of trailers. I could outfit one with all the required legal components, down to hot and cold running water, and drive to customers instead of having them come to me. I was very clear from the beginning about not wanting it to look like a taco truck; why re-create something that's already being done perfectly?

It took me and Danny, my business partner at the time, a while to figure out our model. It's one thing if I'm selling the same taco or the same crepes every day. There's a reason so many people do that. It's predictable, you know exactly what you're purchasing, and all that stuff. But what we wanted was to change every day—location, menu, specials. It would be a moving target. I did want a simple core comfort food menu of staples and to elaborate from there. We started with a signature Kobe-style beef burger with bacon jam, arugula, and blue cheese on a locally made roll.

I stumbled upon a trailer up in Arlington, Washington, about an hour north of Seattle. The guy wanted $10,000 for a 1962 silver Airstream that was fairly empty, except that it did have a commercial hood and a three-compartment sink. It took me six months to talk him down, but I finally got him to agree to a $5,000 selling price, which was all that (maybe more than) I could afford. We outfitted it with a four-burner range, a fryer, a pan chiller, and a fridge, and we were halfway there. The plan was to drive the trailer to a different neighborhood each day, sometimes more than one, alerting people where to find us through our website and through tools like Google Maps and Twitter, which were just barely taking off back then.

We originally wanted to call the business Le Pigeon and had a logo and everything mocked up to launch, but then a fantastic chef, Gabe Rucker, opened a restaurant by the same name down in Portland. So I chose the name of the only tool you ever really need to make a meal (save a few knives): the skillet. I loved the idea of cast iron and the beauty and ruggedness of the pan.

I was still concerned about how we were going to get our name out there. It's hard to remember now, when high-end street food is so big that it's almost clichéd, but people in Seattle hadn't seen anything like us before. No one was clamoring for something like it, as far as we knew. The closest thing to what we were planning was the handful of "underground restaurants" around town, hush-hush ventures where you would pay for dinner in a home or another unpermitted space. Like them, we originally tried to operate as a "private club." We would sell lifetime memberships for a buck apiece and only allow members to buy our food. It was a way around not having a permit, and it let some of the underground restaurants squeak by semilegally. The health department initially told me that was an acceptable idea. By the time we had Skillet running, though, they kind of laughed it off and conveniently didn't remember saying that it was OK.

As the spring wore on, I was fairly desperate to get the trailer on the street. I had quit my job and thrown everything into preparations. I'd been feeding local newspapers one-word e-mails about our plans from the beginning of January, and the buzz was happening. I had no prior experience with the media and was blown away by this. I felt like what we were planning was pretty cool, but I thought we'd have to keep muddling around for a while until somebody noticed. I mean, my aunt's been operating a little café in the suburbs for twenty years, called Alexa's, and she is constantly amazed at all the great press we get. Instead, the media all seemed to be interested, and a splashy article on us came out the day we opened.

What the writers didn't know is that we weren't fully permitted to sell food. I had figured it was a bigger risk for me to not pay my bills than to get going and risk getting my hand slapped. And I didn't agree with the rules. Logically, I didn't understand why I was supposed to wait months to get our final paperwork, when it was obvious to me that we were serving food safely—more safely than a number of kitchens I've been in that were, in fact, health department approved.

Looking back, it was selfish of me. Other people are like, "That's the law! I don't break laws!" But the system is so backward. I'd worked in enough permitted operations to know the food safety rules and knew I wasn't going to make anyone sick. I felt like we were ready, I loved our food, and other people said they loved it (though you have to realize that in most any situation, people will tell you they love your food and most of the time that's 50 percent bullshit).

I don't remember a lot about that first day on the streets. Our early days of food prep were done in the kitchen where Danny worked as an equipment representative. Space was tight, and it was a long drive from where we served, but it was all we had. The first day of service we were

in South Lake Union, I remember that much. Currently the neighborhood is booming with corporate headquarters and thousands of office workers, but back then it was a little more industrial and out of the way. I rolled out the truck and parked it in a parking lot. I think we made $200 or $300 that day and I was so nervous—I was so nervous for a long time actually, nervous about a bunch of things.

Money was a big one, because I wasn't living the nomadic bachelor lifestyle anymore. I had met Kelli after moving back to Seattle. I told my mom the first week I met Kelli that I thought I had met my wife, and I think she told the same thing to her mom. We were engaged within nine months. She was just amazing. Amazingly kind and beautiful inside and out. I was also pretty confident she was going to support me, at least within reason, in the crazy ideas I had. As a partner, you've both got to buy into each other.

The first time we served Skillet's burgers, milkshakes, and fries was at our wedding. The trailer wasn't up and running then, but we had grills and cooks and recipes, and each other.

But on the streets, I was nervous about the city cracking down on us. And in a weird way I was nervous about the splash we were making, as much as I'd worked on creating it. National magazines wrote about us early on. We had lines down the block pretty much from the start. People loved the burger and the poutine, the pork belly with waffles and the lemongrass-braised pork. We had a community wherever we went; entire offices would empty out so workers could stand in line together for a lunch date with us. When our credit card machine went down for a few weeks, we just gave people IOUs. Every last person came back to pay up. It was great, and yet it would've been less stressful to ease into this and quietly get our footing.

And then, a few weeks into it, the shoe did drop: the health department stopped by and told us we had to shut down. I had a whole line of fifty people staring at us. I had to ask the inspectors, "What happens if I just keep serving?" I wondered, is it worth it to stay open? What are the consequences? They threatened to have us arrested. For serving burgers. Well, all right then. If I wound up in jail, my wife would be pissed about that.

I had a lot of closed-door meetings with the health department. They didn't like me. I don't blame them: they were trying to do their job; they've got their hoops they have to jump through. We got our papers in order and got back on the streets, though that wasn't our only run-in. We found ourselves shut down more times afterward. As our business has become more stable, we haven't taken risks like that. But let's set one thing straight: we knew what we were doing, the risks we were taking. And I realize the inspectors are just trying to keep the public safe, especially given that they're dealing with a food system that is totally fucked up in this country. They have to manage the mess created by our oversystematized web of food manufacturers and distributors, where we have commoditized and processed our food. But I truly believe that we're oversanitizing America— and creating more ways for diseases to thrive in the process. That to me is where the health department misses the boat.

They often conform to the letter of the law when sometimes the spirit of the law is what's needed. I don't know how this problem is going to be fixed, but I can only hope that it's possible to reverse the intensity with which we industrialized our food from the 1950s on and get back to more regional production with the same fervor.

I don't take safety rules lightly at all. I just feel like if you pay attention to where your ingredients come from, if you know the correct procedures, and if you're a chef who pays attention to the craft, it'll be fine. I'd taken food safety courses and run food operations for years; I knew how to keep the public and my employees safe. But c'mon, people, look at where we're actually seeing the big problems with contaminated food—it's giant industrialized recalls of thirty-six million pounds of turkey and five hundred million eggs. It's not with the food trucks. Let's start bringing the food closer to where we live and take another look at our regulations. I realize it's more expensive, but this is important stuff, and ultimately, if we don't start eating more locally, it'll really cost us in much bigger and worse ways.

I try to do my part with the food I serve. I believe in seasonality. I believe in using local ingredients, or at least regional ones, probably even more than in using organic ingredients. I'm not a big stickler; I'm not going to be out there with tweezers picking petals off a flower in the middle of a rural field to serve on our plates—that's not the price point or the place where we need to land—but I do what I can. The crapshoot is that even being local doesn't mean 100 percent that ingredients are going to be better. You have to know what you're getting—you have to pay attention.

Protein and produce are where we focus. If the majority of that can be local, that's great. Waiting for in-season vegetables can be a little tough sometimes, especially when we have late summers in the Northwest. You're just screaming for corn, and some years it's not going to happen until late August or even September. We have California for those times, which is at least closer than a lot of other places where we could source cheaper food. We have to ask hard questions at times, when the price for the kind of food we want is just too crazy—but what is really crazy? Americans have this mind-set that food should be cheap, but I think food needs to cost what it costs. Everyone has a vision of buying a chicken that's been coddled during its life and gently led to slaughter before it's put on a bun for their sandwich, but the reality is, that costs money.

So that brings us back to the trailer. One early review said our food was the best ten-dollar meal you could ever eat. That was nice, but it unwittingly targeted our main problem. Our food costs were way too high, and we were charging way too little. I just wasn't convinced that the public would spend restaurant prices on the street, and so I waited to raise our prices to reflect our actual costs. That was a drastic mistake. We should have started charging what we needed to from the beginning, and that is truly one of my biggest regrets, as it put us in a hole from day one. Even after we got the correct permit and had lines of a hundred folks for lunch, we weren't making any money.

Living month to month isn't a good thing for a partnership. Skillet has struggled from the get-go financially, but we've survived. A lot of people stay stuck in that spot for ten years—they grind. I wanted to hit stage B—stability, growth—sooner. But I wasn't the easiest person in my early partnerships either. I considered everyone else an investor in my vision. I didn't want to think that anyone else's opinion mattered. I felt Skillet was my baby, my idea that I had shared, an opportunity that hadn't come to me before, ever. And I didn't want to let go. This was finally settled when another investor, Greg, bought out my original business partner, Danny. While the end of that partnership was a tumultuous one, we wouldn't be where we are today without Danny. He was there from the beginning and contributed with his whole heart. Seeing where we are today, though, I know that the business needed Greg. He's good in all the areas I'm not. He stays in the background, he's good at financial reporting, and he knows the details of running a business. Greg streamlined our costs and got Skillet closer to solid ground. That let me stay hyperfocused on the food and on the brand.

At that point we were at a crossroads and a defining moment of growth. Our first thought was to get more trailers. We had expanded to two, but even doubling in size left me feeling like the business had gotten diluted and overextended. We're not a street-food truck that does the same thing all the time. I wasn't willing to expand if it meant training cooks to cook the same five recipes every day. And we still didn't have a handle on labor costs. The tricky thing about street food is that, when you send a trailer out into the city, it needs three people. You have to commit to staffing for the whole day, and you base the staffing on projected sales. So it's kind of like legalized gambling: you roll the dice every day, guessing the length of the lines and the number of orders at each venue. You can't cut someone midshift and tell them to take the bus home.

The summer of 2008 was crazy busy. Neighborhoods, especially ones that didn't have great restaurants of their own, were asking us to add stops. And despite all that, we still didn't turn a profit.

We put ourselves into hibernation late in 2008. Winters are hard anyway in this city. In downtown Seattle, on a sunny day, we would kill it. But on a rainy day it's anyone's game, and winter means day after day, week after week, of rainy days. Greg thought the hibernation was the end of it: that was it, we'd tried our best, and it was time to close up shop. From an accountant's perspective, we should have. But I couldn't let go just yet. Clearly we had tapped into something new and exciting. I didn't want to be just a blip on the scene.

The Powers That Be must have wanted us to stick around too. One night Kelli and I had a conversation in which we started talking seriously about shutting it all down and walking away. We had a newborn son and knew something needed to change if we were going to make it. The very next week though, we caught a break: a flood of online sales of our packaged Bacon Jam from national gift guides. That infusion of cash stabilized the business. We started hauling the trucks back out in the spring, and our sales were through the roof. It was a vindicating return from

hibernation to see blocks-long lines greeting us. We were doing something right, and the city missed us when we were gone.

Today, Skillet is both a mobile restaurant and a brick-and-mortar diner. We still serve burgers downtown from the trailer at lunch, but we now also have a bustling space on Capitol Hill, complete with green vinyl booths and heavy diner coffee mugs. Magazines call us one of the pioneers in what's become a national craze. Seattle has pods of street-food trucks congregating around town—and ironically, for a guy who started out breaking the rules, I get asked for advice all the time by people looking to start up new businesses. I'm always more than willing to talk with them if they seem serious. The city has enacted some new laws that make it easier to sell food and serve customers; they're real game-changers. Some of the new trucks will fail, but I can tell that some of them have the food and the ideas and the commitment and the panache to make it work.

Here's what I can tell them: the restaurant business is not for the faint of heart. It will kick your ass. But if you can stick it out, you'll absolutely see the happy ending.

It might be the sight of 150 friends and family walking through the doors of your first diner to celebrate your success. It might be seeing a stiff-collared businessman plop down on the sidewalk to dive into a big box of poutine on his lunch break. When you have these moments, it's all worth it. I do what I do because I believe in the power of good food. I believe everyone should be able to enjoy it, and if that means we drive to you, so be it. Skillet was born of passion and sweat and tears and endless support from so many people. I am eternally thankful for their belief in this business and am so looking forward to where we go next. Keep your Google Maps open—we'll keep you posted.

breakfast

Pancakes with
Rhubarb Compote and
Lemon-Zested Butter

Leavened Cornmeal Waffle
with Braised Pork Belly
and Sunny-Side Egg

Cinnamon Brioche French Toast

Cauliflower Scramble

Guanciale with Fried
Egg on Brioche

Buttermilk Biscuits with Chicken
Sausage and Sage Gravy

Skillet Granola

MORNINGS IN SEATTLE can vary depending on the weather. On bright summer mornings we're all awake and cheery, and we seem to have lived half a day by 8:30 a.m. We wave hello, we smile at neighbors, and we talk about the weather. Always, we talk about the weather. We take pictures of Mount Rainier with our phones as we cross I-90—that's how much we love the sunshine. If it's raining, well, there may be no smiles or waves, but we're still talking about the weather. We walk to our favorite coffee shop and talk about our hopes for sunshine over the weekend and the next time it'll get above 70 degrees.

No matter what the weather, though, one thing's for sure: we're all drinking coffee. It's a morning ritual for the Seattleite. No matter what form it comes in, you can be sure we have our opinions and favorites. At the diner, we serve Fonté Coffee, from a little coffee roaster run by nice people who pay a lot of attention to their beans. The coffee isn't as sexy as some of the bigger indie brands in town. It's even a little fuddy-duddy—they serve it at the Four Seasons hotels. But I don't feel like I need to toe the line for image. The bottom line is, I drink Fonté at home, and it's what I like.

Coffee cannot stand alone, though. It's not the same without your eggs, toast, pastry, or fruit. We at Skillet believe breakfast should be taken slow. We did breakfast at the trailer for a year or so. It meant getting up at 4 a.m. to prep the eggs, the granola, the waffles, and the pork belly. Some of my fondest memories are seeing our regulars ride up on their bikes on the way to work. They parked, ordered a heaping pile of pork belly and waffle, and sat to enjoy every bite. Knowing they were full and satisfied before their day had even begun left me feeling just as happy. And their breakfast wasn't an on-the-fly piece of toast: it was hearty, it was heaping, it was . . . well, not exactly the healthiest, but oh so good.

The Skillet Diner serves breakfast all day. That's how much we like it. We think bacon, pork belly, waffles, pancake stacks, and large bowls of yogurt and granola should be a part of your everyday lives. That's what diners are for—to belly up to the bar and have your coffee in a heavy mug with a big breakfast. So what better way to start our book than with the foundation of all that is good and holy on the breakfast menu: the pancake.

pancakes with rhubarb compote and lemon-zested butter

||||||||||||||||||||||||||||||||||||||||||||||||||||||||||||||||||||||||||||||||||||||||||||||||||||||||||||||||

Makes 8 to 12 pancakes

Pancakes are the cornerstone of the morning meal. They're nostalgic and comforting, as easily dressed up as dressed down. In this case, any of our additions would enhance your basic pancake, but we think you can't beat putting them all together: the sweet-tart luxury of compote and compound butter and homemade syrup. It looks complex, but none of the parts take long to assemble and cook. Make the syrup and compote ahead of time if you like.

1. Put the milk, buttermilk, melted butter, and eggs in a blender and blend on medium-high for about a minute, until nice and frothy. In a medium bowl, sift together the flour, baking powder, salt, and sugar. Add the dry ingredients to the blender and mix until just smooth. Mix in the vanilla. Let the batter rest for 10 to 15 minutes.

1 cup whole milk

1 cup buttermilk

¼ cup (½ stick) unsalted butter, melted and cooled to room temperature, plus extra to coat the skillet

2 large eggs, beaten

2 cups all-purpose flour, scooped into a measuring cup and leveled with a knife

¼ cup baking powder

1 teaspoon kosher salt

¼ cup sugar

¼ teaspoon vanilla extract

1 cup Rhubarb Compote (page 7)

¼ cup plus 2 tablespoons Lemon-Zested Butter (page 7)

1 cup Homemade Syrup (page 8)

2. Heat a medium skillet or griddle over medium-high heat until a few sprinkles of water splatter when dropped on the surface. Put a few teaspoons of butter in the pan and melt until slightly foamy, swirling the pan to coat with the melted butter. Using a small ladle or scoop, pour about ¼ cup of batter onto the skillet for each pancake, spacing them a few inches apart. When bubbles start to appear on the top, in 2 to 3 minutes, flip them over. Cook them for another 1 to 2 minutes, until lightly browned.

3. Repeat with the remaining batter, brushing the pan with melted butter between batches.

4. To serve, stack 3 pancakes on each plate, putting a tablespoon or so of the compote between each cake. Top with a little lemon-zested butter and drizzle with syrup.

RHUBARB COMPOTE

Makes about 1 cup

1 tablespoon butter

1 cup sliced rhubarb

¼ cup sugar

1. Heat a sauté pan on medium heat. Add the butter and let it melt until it is lightly foaming, 30 to 60 seconds. Add the rhubarb and sugar, mix until the rhubarb is coated, and cook until soft, about 10 minutes. Add a tablespoon or two of water if needed to keep the compote from sticking. Set aside until ready to use.

LEMON-ZESTED BUTTER

Makes about ½ cup

½ cup (1 stick) butter, at room temperature

Zest of 1 medium lemon (about 2 teaspoons)

¾ teaspoon freshly squeezed lemon juice

1½ teaspoons confectioners' sugar

Pinch of kosher salt

1. Using a hand mixer or a whisk, whip all the ingredients together in a medium bowl until fluffy. Set aside until ready to use.

¼ cup plus 2 tablespoons (packed) light brown sugar

2 tablespoons granulated sugar

¼ cup plus 2 tablespoons water

¼ cup organic light corn syrup

½ cinnamon stick

¼ teaspoon vanilla extract

Pinch of salt

HOMEMADE SYRUP

Makes about 1 cup

1. Combine all the ingredients in a large saucepan and bring to a simmer. Simmer for about 10 minutes, remove and discard the cinnamon stick, and set aside until ready to use.

The Science of Pancakes

YOU WANT PANCAKES to be light and fluffy. The easiest way to achieve this is by using baking powder and an acid, like buttermilk, to make a chemical reaction that produces carbon dioxide. When released, the carbon dioxide creates bubbles within the batter and makes the final product lighter. You'll see the same thing in breads that have yeast in the dough. The yeast makes carbon dioxide, just like baking powder does—though in lower amounts—and creates lighter breads. You need the reaction to happen quickly, as the pancakes are cooked pretty quickly in a skillet, compared to bread, which cooks in an oven for a much longer time.

There are other ways you can create a lighter pancake. One is to use a blender—just place all the wet ingredients into it and blend on high for a minute until frothy. Then add the dry ingredients and pulse until all the ingredients are incorporated. Remove the batter from the blender and allow it to sit for 10 to 20 minutes before using. Again, the idea is to add air and make the batter nice and light.

Another thing you can do is to separate the eggs. Follow our master recipe, except that when it calls for adding the eggs, just add the beaten yolks. Then, at the end of the recipe, just before you're ready to cook the pancakes, whisk the egg whites to stiff peaks and fold them gently into the batter. I use this method to make light pancakes when I don't have any buttermilk (be sure to add an equal amount of whole milk to the recipe to substitute for the missing buttermilk).

No matter which method you choose, follow one simple rule: *Do not overmix the ingredients!* Just incorporate them together. The more you mix, the more gluten will form, which will create a dense batter and in turn a heavy pancake.

A few other pancake tips:

Melt the butter in a microwave on defrost for a few seconds to start the melting process. The butter will start to melt but won't be too hot. Once it starts melting, you can remove it from the microwave and swish it around till it's all melted.

Make sure all the ingredients are at room temperature before you start mixing. The melted butter will surely solidify again if it contacts cold milk. The warmer temperature also helps the baking powder react in a stronger way to produce more carbon dioxide.

Check the expiration date on your baking powder before using it. Old baking powder loses its potency.

Understand that you may not know how your skillet and heat source really react to the pancake recipe until you try one. Use caution and your nose to see if the pancakes are burning. Adjust the temperature accordingly. I believe the first pancake is always a tester and should be sacrificed to the one cooking the breakfast!

leavened cornmeal waffle with braised pork belly and sunny-side egg

Makes 4 to 5 waffles

The showstopper of all breakfasts, our pork belly and waffle will wow the folks at your breakfast table. The smell alone will stop them in their tracks, and upon plating, it's tough to wait for the fork. The dish is savory-sweet, an indulgence, but it—along with our burger—was one of the original dishes on the truck that people consistently went crazy over.

The idea came from an amazing brunch I had at Le Pigeon in Portland. They were doing a dish with waffles and a braise on top. I think they were using something wild like offal; to me pork belly sounded just great. Putting all these components together involves a lot of advance planning, but it pays off: you don't wait until Sunday morning to cure a pork belly for Sunday brunch, but once you take a day to cure a batch, it'll supply you for many meals.

We use a yeasted waffle that involves creating a sourdough starter (Skillet Orange-Rye Starter on page 15).

FOR THE LEVAIN:

¼ cup Skillet Orange-Rye Starter (page 15)

1¾ cups warm water (80 to 90 degrees F)

3½ cups 50-50 Flour Blend (page 17)

FOR THE WAFFLE BATTER:

½ cup whole milk

2 tablespoons butter, melted

2 eggs, beaten

¼ cup plus 2 tablespoons all-purpose flour

¼ cup plus 2 tablespoons pastry flour

2 tablespoons cornmeal

3 tablespoons cornstarch

2 tablespoons sugar

continued

1¼ teaspoons salt

2¼ teaspoons vanilla extract

FOR ASSEMBLY:

8 ounces Pork Belly (page 17)

4 Sunny-Side Eggs (page 20)

That also takes an initial time investment—a couple of minutes a day over eight days—but once you put in that work, you'll have a starter you can use for waffles or breads whenever you want, adding great character to your food. A starter is like a complex wine: when you develop a live food over time, you create all sorts of different flavors. The starter is mixed with flour into a levain, *which is sort of an intermediate step between the starter and the loaf. The levain is proofed and then mixed with eggs, more flour, and other ingredients to make the final batter. You can substitute a less intensely flavored waffle to serve with the pork belly and eggs, but I hope you'll give ours a try.*

1. To prepare the *levain*, the day before you want to serve your waffles, combine the starter and water in a large bowl. Gently whisk together just to incorporate until the starter is dissolved and then add the flour blend. Mix again until the *levain* is smooth with no lumps. Cover the bowl with plastic wrap and allow the *levain* to rise in a draft-free place for 4 to 6 hours, or until it has developed a large amount of bubbles. To test if it's ready, fill a container with warm water. Scoop out a teaspoon of the *levain* and drop it into the water. If the *levain* floats, it's ready. If it sinks to the

bottom, it hasn't developed enough and needs to ferment longer. You should have about 4 cups.

2. To prepare the waffle batter, warm the milk in a small saucepan to take the chill off (aim for about 80 degrees F when measured with an instant-read thermometer). In a large bowl, mix the milk with ¼ cup of the *levain* until the it is dissolved. (You can refrigerate the rest of the *levain* to make waffles another day; it should last for a week.) Add the butter and eggs and whisk together. In a separate large bowl, whisk together the all-purpose and pastry flours, cornmeal, cornstarch, sugar, and salt, making sure there are no clumps. In three batches, add the flour mixture to the milk mixture, stirring just to combine after each addition. Mix in the vanilla. Cover the batter with plastic wrap and refrigerate overnight.

3. To assemble the dish, preheat the oven to 350 degrees F.

4. Place the pork belly strips in a roasting pan and add any reserved braising liquid. Place the pan in the oven and heat through, about 8 minutes.

5. While the pork belly heats, make the waffles. Warm a waffle iron as directed. Scoop 2 to 3 ounces of the batter onto the iron, using a small ladle or ice cream scoop and cook until golden brown, about 5 minutes.

6. Place a waffle on each plate with an egg on top, then add a piece of pork belly off to the side, but still on top of, the waffle. Simmer any braising liquid left over from the pork belly until it is slightly reduced, about 3 minutes. Skim any foam off the top, and spoon it like a syrup over everything.

SKILLET ORANGE-RYE STARTER

Makes 5½ cups

1. **Day 1:** In a 1-quart container, mix ½ cup of the orange juice, ¼ cup of the rye flour, and ¼ cup of the whole wheat flour to form a thick paste. Place a towel over the container and place it in an area free from drafts and direct sunlight.

2. **Day 2:** Add another ½ cup orange juice, ¼ cup rye flour, and ¼ cup whole wheat flour to the original mixture, and stir again to form a paste. Cover and return the container to its resting place.

3. **Day 3:** Repeat day 2.

4. **Day 4:** Repeat day 2. (By this time, you should start seeing some bubbles forming. This is the yeast in action.)

5. **Day 5:** Remove ¾ cup of the starter and place it into a new 1-quart container, discarding the remainder. Add ¾ cup room temperature water and mix until the starter is dissolved. Add ¾ cup of the 50-50 flour blend to the starter mixture and mix. If needed, add more flour, 1 to 2 tablespoons at a time, to form a

2 cups orange juice, divided

1 cup rye flour, divided

1 cup whole wheat flour, divided

1½ cups plus a few table-spoons 50-50 Flour Blend (page 17)

1 teaspoon apple cider vinegar (if needed)

thick paste. Cover and return the container to its resting place.

6. Day 6: Repeat day 5. By this time, you should see more bubbles forming as you allow the starter to feed on the flour. The entire mass should rise by about 20 percent and then deflate as the day goes on. If it doesn't rise, add a teaspoon of apple cider vinegar to the mix.

7. Day 7: Repeat day 5.

8. Day 8: The starter should be ready to use. It should look alive—you should see bubbles in it. To keep it going indefinitely, continue the day 5 routine each day. Any day you want to use your starter, use the remainder (the part you would have otherwise discarded) to begin the *levain* for the waffles or start making sourdough breads or anything else that calls for *levain*. The longer you continue to feed your starter, the more its flavor and stability will develop.

50-50 FLOUR BLEND

Makes 2 pounds

1 pound whole wheat flour

1 pound all-purpose flour

1. Combine well in a large container. Set aside.

PORK BELLY

Makes 4 pounds

1. To prepare the cure, preheat a small skillet over medium heat. Mix the sugar and salt in a medium bowl; set aside. Add the juniper berries, cloves, cinnamon sticks, and peppercorns to the skillet and toast until they are fragrant, 5 to 8 minutes. Keep a careful eye on them so they don't burn. Allow the toasted spices to cool a bit and then put them in a small spice grinder or a mortar and coarsely grind. Combine the ground spices with the sugar and salt mix.

2. Cover the bottom of a large pan with the cure mixture, and roll the pork belly in it until it is thoroughly coated. Cut the belly into 3-by-4-inch pieces and put them in 1 or 2 gallon-size resealable plastic bags. Refrigerate for at least 12 hours and up to 2 days.

FOR THE CURE:

½ cup sugar

¼ cup kosher salt

5 juniper berries

5 whole cloves

3 cinnamon sticks

1 teaspoon black peppercorns

4 pounds pork belly

FOR THE BRAISING LIQUID:

1 quart chicken stock

1 quart apple juice

1 cup loosely packed dark brown sugar

3 cinnamon sticks

3 sprigs fresh thyme

3. Remove the belly pieces from the bags and wipe off any remaining cure. Preheat a large skillet over medium heat. Place the belly in the pan with the fat side down, keeping it to one pan if possible. The idea is to render some fat from the belly before you braise it, so turn the heat down as needed to avoid browning. You can also weigh the belly down with a cast-iron skillet so the pieces cook more evenly. After a few minutes, when most of the fat has been rendered, remove the belly pieces and set them aside. Carefully drain the fat into a container and discard it.

4. Preheat the oven to 350 degrees F.

5. To prepare the braising liquids, put all the ingredients into a large pot and bring to a boil. Whisk until the sugar dissolves. Pour the liquid (including the cinnamon sticks and thyme sprigs) carefully into a large, deep roasting pan, filling it 1 to 2 inches deep. Place the belly pieces into the pan and ladle off liquid as needed, reserving the excess, until only about the bottom third of the belly remains submerged. Place the pan in the oven and cook for 1½ to 2 hours, or until the pieces are fork-tender. Check from time to

time and add more of the reserved liquid as needed to keep the lower third of the belly covered.

6. Remove the belly pieces and transfer them to a large container with high sides. Strain the braising liquid to remove the cinnamon sticks and thyme sprigs. Pour the strained liquid over the belly strips and refrigerate for up to 7 days. A cap of fat will form on top. Remove the fat and discard it when you are ready to use the belly.

4 teaspoons butter

4 eggs

Salt and freshly ground
pepper

SUNNY-SIDE EGGS

Makes 4 eggs

1. Heat a large skillet over high heat. Let it sit for about
   20 seconds, then reduce the heat to medium-low. Melt
   1 teaspoon of butter in the skillet until it's frothy but
   not burned. Crack an egg right into the butter and
   season to taste with salt and pepper. Swirl the pan
   to make sure the egg isn't sticking. Cook it until the
   edges crisp and the middle of the whites are cooked.
   (If you want to speed it up, you can cover the pan, but
   I think that's kind of cheating. Just make sure the
   heat is low enough—you almost can't have it too low,
   but you *can* have it too high.) Repeat with the remaining eggs.

cinnamon brioche french toast

Makes 5 pieces

The key to a delicious french toast is how long you soak the bread in the custard mixture. Most people think just a good dunking will do the trick. Take your time and let it soak for at least 15 minutes before throwing it in the pan for a sumptuous breakfast.

1. Preheat the oven to 325 degrees F.

2. In a large bowl, thoroughly blend the milk, cream, eggs, sugar, cinnamon, vanilla and salt. Pour the custard into a large casserole pan. Place the brioche slices in the custard, making sure to cover each slice, and soak for 15 minutes. (Do this in stages if they won't all fit.)

3. Preheat the oven to 325 degrees F.

4. Heat a large ovenproof skillet over medium heat and add the butter to the pan. (Make sure the pan is not so hot that the butter burns.) Allow the butter to

1½ cups whole milk

1½ cups heavy cream

7 large eggs, lightly beaten

½ cup sugar

1 tablespoon ground cinnamon

1 tablespoon vanilla extract

½ teaspoon salt

5 thick slices brioche

1 tablespoon butter

melt, and swirl the pan to coat the bottom with the butter. Gently place 2 brioche slices (or however many will fit without crowding) into the pan and cook for approximately 1 minute, or until golden brown. Flip the slices, transfer the pan to the oven, and bake for an additional 3 minutes or until the center is firm.

cauliflower scramble

Makes 6 servings

When we first started Skillet, we'd just do a breakfast scramble with whatever we had on hand, but I kept gravitating toward cauliflower. I'm a big fan—I think it's underutilized and should replace tofu as a go-to for vegetarians. It's got some great qualities that both vegetarians and meat-eaters love. The texture is meaty and firm, and when you caramelize it, it gets so sweet and nice. No matter what additions you use, here's the key to a good scramble: when you think the eggs are 70 percent cooked, turn the heat off and let the rest cook residually. You want the eggs to flow, not clump together—this isn't an egg pancake. I like the ratio here of vegetables to eggs, but you can adjust it to your tastes.

1. Heat two cast-iron or heavy-bottomed skillets over medium heat: one for the scramble and the other for grilling the toast.

2 tablespoons olive oil

6 ounces bacon, thinly sliced (about 6 strips, or ½ cup julienned)

12 ounces cauliflower (about half of a large head), cut into small florets

12 ounces Yukon Gold potatoes (about 4), cut into small dice

4 ounces shallot (about 2 large), minced

Salt and freshly ground pepper

10 large eggs, beaten

2 tablespoons Crème Fraîche (page 26)

2 tablespoons minced chives, divided

4 tablespoons (½ stick) butter

6 slices thick rustic bread

2. Add the olive oil and bacon to the pan you'll use for the scramble. Cook the bacon until it starts to color but hasn't started to crisp, about 3 minutes. Using a slotted spoon or spatula, remove the bacon from the pan and reserve. Remove all but 1 tablespoon of the fat from the pan. Return the pan to the heat and warm it back up.

3. Once the pan is warmed, add the cauliflower, potatoes, shallots, and salt and pepper to taste. The goal here is not just to cook these ingredients but to caramelize them. In order to do this, you need to maintain a good temperature: adjust the heat either up or down, depending on how the vegetables are cooking. You want them to develop a nice coppery color, but not burn. As their water evaporates, the vegetables may start to stick to the bottom. That's perfectly fine— just scrape them with a wooden spoon or spatula and add a little water as needed. When they are nearly done, which may take up to 15 minutes, return the bacon to the pan to finish cooking.

4. Once the bacon has crisped, about 2 minutes, reduce the heat to medium-low and add the eggs to the pan. Cook them with all the other ingredients until they

are barely soft scrambled, about 6 minutes. Do not cook the eggs all the way through. Remove the pan from the heat and fold in the crème fraîche and 1 tablespoon chives. Set the scramble aside for a moment to let the residual heat finish cooking the eggs.

5. In the other pan, melt the butter over medium heat. Swirl the pan to coat it with the butter. Turn the heat up to medium-high and add the bread to the pan. If the butter isn't covering the entire surface of the slices, add a little more. Toast the bread in the pan until the bottom is golden brown, 2 to 4 minutes. Carefully flip the bread over and continue to toast for another 2 to 4 minutes. Remove the bread from the pan and set aside.

6. Warm 6 plates. On each plate, place a piece of toast, buttered side up. Spoon the scramble on top of the bread, allowing it to overflow and fall down a little. Garnish the scramble with the remaining tablespoon of chives and serve.

1 cup heavy cream

Juice of 1 medium lemon
(about 2 teaspoons)

CRÈME FRAÎCHE

Makes 1 cup

*It's OK to use store-bought crème fraîche, but why would
you? It's not hard to make it at home; the flavor is fresher
and tangier and more complex, and the price is a lot easier to handle.*

1. Mix the cream and lemon juice in a clean container.
   Place in a warm spot (80 to 85 degrees F is ideal) for
   a few days, to allow the cream to thicken. Check each
   day and stir as needed, until the cream has thickened
   to a custardy consistency. (Don't worry if your room
   is cooler, even as low as 65 degrees F; the process
   will just take longer.) Once the cream has thickened,
   refrigerate the container and use within a week.

guanciale with fried egg on brioche

Makes 4 sandwiches

This is how we do an American breakfast sandwich, Skillet-style. Guanciale *is the Italian name for cured pork jowls, which are simple to make at home so long as you have some time and some refrigerator space. You don't even need a smoker; you're just curing the meat in your fridge. Look for the jowls at butcher shops, or try a well-stocked Asian or Mexican market. The recipe makes a lot, but it keeps well, and you'll be glad to have a supply on hand—make a BLT out of some of the extras and people will be blown away.*

12 slices Guanciale (page 29)

4 brioche buns, split

3 tablespoons butter

4 large eggs

4 slices American cheese

1. Preheat the oven to 350 degrees F.

2. Place the guanciale on a baking sheet fitted with a cooking rack; bake for 15 to 20 minutes, or until it has rendered some of its fat and is golden brown and crispy. Toast the buns in a dry pan for a minute or two over medium heat, until golden brown. Melt the butter in a large skillet over medium heat, swirl the

pan to coat it with the butter, and crack the eggs into the pan. Fry the eggs until the whites crisp at the edges and are cooked in the middle, about 3 minutes, and transfer the fried eggs with a slotted spoon to the toasted buns. Top each egg with a slice of American cheese and 3 slices of guanciale.

GUANCIALE

Makes 3 pounds

The spices in this guanciale are what skew it toward breakfast. Commonly, hard spices such as whole cloves and allspice berries sit on your shelves for a long time without being used. Even if you purchased them recently, you really never know how long they may have been sitting at the store. Given that, if we were to just grind the spices without toasting them first, the flavors would likely be bland. We want to wake up the spices and bring out their oils first. This is a good habit to get into when using any hard spice.

¾ cup salt

¾ cup sugar

1½ cinnamon sticks

1 tablespoon whole cloves

1 tablespoon allspice berries

1 tablespoon black peppercorns

Leaves from ½ bunch fresh thyme (about 1½ ounces), chopped

3 pounds (about 2 large) fresh pork jowls

1. Combine the salt and sugar in a large bowl. In a small sauté pan over medium-low heat, add the cinnamon sticks, cloves, allspice berries, and peppercorns. Toast the spices for a minute or two, shaking the pan until they're fragrant. Remove them from the heat and allow to cool slightly. Using a spice grinder or a mortar and pestle, grind the spices in batches. Add them to the bowl with the salt and sugar. Add the thyme leaves, and thoroughly combine.

2. To prepare the pork jowls, trim off any bloody bits or other extraneous tissue. Spread a thick layer of the cure on the bottom of a large roasting pan or other large pan. Working with one jowl at a time, place the jowl on top of the cure. Sprinkle more cure onto the jowl to cover it entirely, then transfer it into a 1-gallon resealable plastic bag. Squeeze the air from the bag and seal the top. Repeat the process with the remaining jowl.

3. Place the bagged jowls on a large plate in the refrigerator. Wait 2 days. Turn the jowls over, rubbing the cure through the plastic to recoat as needed. You'll notice liquid building up within the bag, which is normal. Repeat this process until the jowls have been curing for 8 to 10 days and feel much firmer than when you began. Remove them from the bags, discard the bags, and brush off any excess cure. Place a rack on top of a large platter or baking sheet. Put the jowls on top of the rack, cover, and refrigerate for another day or two, or until the jowls are dried. When the jowls have dried, slice them into ⅛-inch-thick

strips, similar to bacon. Share the extra guanciale with your friends or reserve for future use—it freezes well in a resealable plastic bag. Make sure to squeeze any extra air out of the bag before sealing it to avoid freezer burn.

buttermilk biscuits with chicken sausage and sage gravy

1 tablespoon olive oil

1 pound Chicken Sausage
(page 33)

1⅓ cups Sage Gravy
(page 34)

8 Big B's Biscuits (page 36)

Handful of fresh sage leaves,
for garnish

Makes 4 servings

This is not a meal for the faint of heart. The chicken sausage is spiced with cardamom, which adds an unexpected kick to the traditional sausage spice mixture. The gravy is dressed up with the addition of sage. The biscuits are big. Pile it all together and you've got a hearty start to the day.

1. Heat the olive oil in a heavy skillet or other heavy-bottomed pan over medium-high heat. Brown the chicken sausage aggressively, stirring occasionally. Scrape the browned bits off the bottom of the pan as the sausage is cooking. Once it is cooked through, add the gravy to the pan and mix all together. If you made the gravy earlier and are reheating it, warm it over low heat until heated through.

2. Put 2 biscuits on each of 4 warm plates or bowls. Ladle about ⅓ cup of gravy with chicken sausage over the biscuits, until the tops are covered. Garnish with sage leaves.

CHICKEN SAUSAGE

Makes 2½ pounds

1. In a stand mixer fitted with the paddle attachment, add all the ingredients. Mix on low speed until everything is thoroughly incorporated. If you're making Buttermilk Biscuits with Chicken Sausage and Sage Gravy, reserve 1 pound of the sausage. Divide the rest into portions and freeze them in small resealable plastic bags for future use. Alternatively, if you want to freeze the sausage in a form that can be easily sliced, put a long piece of plastic wrap on the counter and place half the mixture on top. Then fold the plastic over the chicken to form a cylinder (think of those sausage rolls you see at markets). Keep forming the cylinder by rolling it over and over till the sausage is tight and together. Repeat the process with the other half of the mixture.

½ teaspoon ground cinnamon

½ teaspoon ground cardamom

½ teaspoon ground allspice

½ teaspoon coarsely ground black pepper

½ teaspoon rubbed dried sage

¼ teaspoon ground cloves

1½ tablespoons kosher salt

½ cup ice-cold water

2½ pounds ground chicken

1 bunch fresh sage (3 to 4 ounces)

2 cups whole milk

½ cup (1 stick) butter

½ cup all-purpose flour

Salt and freshly ground pepper

SAGE GRAVY

Makes about 2 cups

This fragrant gravy can be made ahead of time. It will last in the fridge up to three days.

1. Chop 1 tablespoon sage leaves and set aside. Add the remaining sage, together with the milk, to a small saucepan. Bring them to a boil and immediately remove from the heat. Allow the leaves to steep in the milk for 10 to 15 minutes, almost as if you were making tea. Strain the milk, discard the sage leaves, and reserve.

2. Heat a large skillet or other heavy-bottomed pan over medium-high heat. Add the butter and allow it to melt completely. Add the flour to the pan and whisk it with the butter to form a roux. *Be careful—the contents from here on out will be very hot!* Keep whisking the roux until it gives off a nutty aroma, 3 to 5 minutes. It will have changed color at this point, from very light and blond to more like the color of a wet, sandy

beach. Add the reserved chopped sage. Using small ladlefuls, start adding the sage-flavored milk to the roux. *Did we mention that the contents will be hot? Please use extreme caution.* Once all the milk has been added, whisk until the gravy is smooth and lump free. Season to taste with salt and pepper.

3 cups all-purpose flour

1 cup pastry flour

1½ tablespoons kosher salt

1 tablespoon baking powder

1 teaspoon baking soda

1 cup (2 sticks) butter, cut into small dice and chilled as cold as possible without freezing

1½ cups buttermilk, cold, plus extra for basting the biscuits

BIG B'S BISCUITS

Makes about 1 dozen big biscuits

Like most biscuits, these are best when they're fresh. But they're really still pretty good a day or two later, so make them in advance if you must and reheat them to serve.

1. Preheat the oven to 425 degrees F.

2. In a large bowl, mix the all-purpose and pastry flours, salt, baking powder, and baking soda. Mix the butter into the flour mixture, either using a pastry cutter or rubbing it gently between your fingers, working as fast as possible to break down the butter into pea-size pieces. Do not overmix the ingredients, as you're trying to avoid developing the gluten within the flour, which will make the biscuits tough.

3. Make a well in the center of the mixture and pour the buttermilk into it, quickly mixing it in with a fork. Don't completely incorporate the buttermilk; stop as soon as the dough holds together in a shaggy mass. Transfer the dough onto a lightly floured surface and press down with your fingers to form a 9-by-12-inch rectangle—it doesn't have to be exactly to size, so long

as the dough is fairly even and no more than ¼ inch thick. Using a 2- to 3-inch cookie cutter or a floured glass, cut the biscuits out and place them on a baking sheet lined with a Silpat mat or parchment paper. Bake the biscuits halfway, about 8 minutes. Remove the baking sheet from the oven. Using a pastry brush, baste each biscuit with buttermilk, or spoon some buttermilk over each one. Return the sheet to the oven for another 8 minutes, or until the biscuits are a dark golden brown.

4. If you have leftover dough, you can reshape it and cut out more biscuits. This second batch will be denser and not as flaky, but will still taste great with jam.

skillet granola

4 cups rolled oats

1 cup wheat germ

1 cup canola oil

¾ cup loosely packed dark brown sugar

¼ cup plus 2 tablespoons honey

1 tablespoon whole milk

1 teaspoon salt

1 teaspoon vanilla extract

1 teaspoon ground cinnamon

1 teaspoon ground cloves

½ cup toasted hazelnuts, chopped

½ cup toasted walnuts, chopped

½ cup golden raisins

½ cup dried cranberries

Makes about 9 cups

Not everyone can eat pork belly and waffles or biscuits and gravy for breakfast. And not everyone who can eat these things wants to eat them every day. For those folks, we offer classic granola, which has all the delicious flavors that come with a savory meal, but in lighter form. Skillet's granola is the perfect topping for plain or vanilla yogurt, and it's great just served with milk. (I mix both applesauce and milk with mine. I don't know why, but I've done it my whole life.) My mom, Barb, is the catalyst for this recipe— it was what we grew up on, really, and it had an amazing smell baking in the oven. My son, Huxley, enjoys it now. He eats it plain as a snack.

1. Preheat the oven to 350 degrees F.

2. Mix the oats and wheat germ together in a large bowl. In a large saucepan over medium heat, simmer the canola oil, brown sugar, honey, milk, salt, vanilla, cinnamon, and cloves for 3 minutes.

3. Pour the hot mixture over the oats and wheat germ. Stir until the grains are evenly coated and then allow the oat mixture to cool slightly. When it has cooled, spread it out onto two baking sheets; the key is to make sure the layers are no more than ½ inch thick; otherwise, the granola will not brown evenly. Bake, stirring occasionally, for 15 to 20 minutes, or until the granola has browned. Let it cool, then break the pieces into a large bowl and mix in the nuts, raisins, and cranberries. It will keep 2 to 3 weeks if stored in an airtight container.

lunch

Crab Cake Po'boy
with Lemon "Aioli"

Lemongrass Pork with
Ginger "Aioli" and Spicy Pickled
Cabbage Slaw

Fried Chicken Sandwich with
Pickled Jalapeño "Aioli"

Egg Salad Sandwich

Duck Tacos

Chicken Salad

Skillet Poutine

"Aiolis"

WEEKDAY LUNCHES are what made Skillet. Weekends were always going to be hit-and-miss with Seattle's weather, and I decided early on that we weren't going to do the late-night greasy food thing. In reality, I didn't want to work late nights. As a restaurant cook, that's a necessary evil, part of the hard grind of kitchen work. Running my own truck means that I get to pick my hours. But also, most nighttime street-food carts park outside concert venues. That's how they make the big bucks, feeding drunk kids hot dogs or pizza. And I really didn't want to serve food to drunk people who were just looking for an instant grease feast. I felt they wouldn't appreciate it as much.

Lunch is the one meal of the day that has a guaranteed turnout and that people definitely eat at a specific time. For street food we mainly do lunch Monday through Friday from 11 a.m. to 2 p.m. We wanted to have a very tight timeline for people to find us; over the years we found that if they thought we'd always be there, they were somehow less likely to show up. The other reason behind the tight schedule was the time it takes to actually get the food prepped and the trailer on the road. We get to the kitchen at 7:30 a.m., prep for a couple of hours, leave the kitchen at 9:30, get to location by 10, and start serving at 11. We leave the day's location around 2 p.m. or whenever we sell out—which happens more often than some would like. It's 4 p.m. before we finish cleaning up and are done. So from a basic quality-of-life aspect, it's already a ten-hour day just doing the three-hour lunch. Doing more than one meal never made sense to me.

As for the food, arriving at a specific location just once a week has a great appeal for our customers. It becomes a "treat" of sorts to get out and walk to Skillet every Tuesday or Wednesday, or whichever day we're in your neighborhood. Over the years we've moved around and created a few different set locations, and there is, thankfully, always a crowd. We post our locations on our website and on Facebook and Twitter, and the people seem to follow.

One moment that stuck with me was the day a man who seemed quite down and out on his luck came up to me after eating our Skillet Burger (page 87). He told me he didn't get to eat food that had great ingredients and flavor very often in his life. I was so honored he ate our food and enjoyed it to the degree that he did. That moment reminded me of why I do what I do, and why I love this street-food life: The streets are for everyone. So is our food.

crab cake po'boy with lemon "aioli"

||||||||||||||||||||||||||||||||||||||||||||||||||||||||||||||||||||||||||||||||||||||||||||||||||||||||||||||||||||||||||||||

Makes 4 sandwiches

This is one of our most requested street-food items whenever we put out the call to "send us your greatest hits." People here in the Northwest have a hard time resisting crab. Dungeness is, I think, the only way to go. I'm biased toward Dungeness because of where we live. It's a little sweeter than most varieties, you get a lot of bang for your buck, and I think it's just a meatier, "crabbier" crab.

1. Melt the butter in a large skillet over medium heat, place the rolls cut side down, and toast until they are golden brown. Spread both sides of the rolls fairly liberally with the aioli. Wipe the skillet clean and heat the grapeseed oil over medium-high heat. Fry the crab cakes, in batches if needed, until they're crispy and brown, about 3 to 4 minutes on each side. If the oil gets dirtied with food debris, or if the level falls below about ¼ inch, replace with clean oil between batches. Place 2 or 3 cakes in each roll, and top with tomatoes and lettuce. Serve immediately.

1 tablespoon butter or oil

4 soft, good-quality sandwich rolls, split

1 cup Lemon "Aioli" (page 46)

¼ cup grapeseed or other neutral oil, plus more as needed

10 to 12 Crab Cakes (page 47)

1 cup sliced roma tomatoes

4 cups iceberg lettuce, cut into julienne strips

1 medium lemon, first zested, then juiced (about 2 teaspoons each)

1 clove garlic, minced

Leaves from 2 sprigs fresh thyme, chopped

3 tablespoons chopped Italian parsley

2 cups mayonnaise

1½ tablespoons honey

Kosher salt and freshly ground pepper

LEMON "AIOLI"

Makes about 2 cups

1. Mix the lemon zest and juice, garlic, thyme leaves, parsley, mayonnaise, and honey in a large bowl. Season to taste with salt and pepper. Transfer the aioli to a clean container and refrigerate for up to a month.

CRAB CAKES

Makes 20 small crab cakes

The key to great crab cakes, besides great crab, is not over-mixing. You want to see some texture to the crab; if you handle it too much it will look like tuna salad. For ours, we use jarred piquillo *peppers—mild, sweet Spanish-style peppers—and Japanese-style panko bread crumbs, which are bigger and flakier than the American version and make for a nice crisp coating. Well-stocked grocery stores should carry both, or you can order them online. We call for cutting some of the crab cake ingredients into a fine dice (the technical term is brunoise, and it means ⅛-inch cubes).*

1 medium shallot, finely diced

1 tablespoon minced Italian parsley

½ tablespoon Dijon-style mustard

1 tablespoon finely diced *piquillo* pepper

½ tablespoon finely diced cornichon or other sour pickle

2 large eggs, lightly beaten

1½ pounds Dungeness crab-meat, picked and drained

1 medium lemon, first zested, then juiced

⅓ cup mayonnaise

⅓ cup panko, plus extra for breading the crab cakes

1 teaspoon freshly ground pepper

½ tablespoon kosher salt

1. Mix all the ingredients together in a large bowl until the mixture barely holds together. This is where you want to be sure not to overmix. Taste to see if the salt and lemon are where they need to be, and adjust the seasonings accordingly. Layer 1 inch of panko in a large baking pan. Form the crab mixture into 20 cakes about 1½ inches in diameter, lightly bread them with the panko, and set them aside. You can either fry them now or refrigerate until ready to use. Don't refrigerate them any longer than 24 hours, and sooner is better.

lemongrass pork with ginger "aioli" and spicy pickled cabbage slaw

||||||||||||||||||||||||||||||||||||||||||||||||||||||||||||||||||||||||||||||||||||||||||||||||||||||||||||||||||

1 pound Lemongrass Pork
(page 49)

4 soft, good-quality buns of
your choice

Butter, for toasting the buns

¼ cup Ginger "Aioli"
(page 50)

¼ cup Spicy Pickled
Cabbage Slaw (page 51)

Makes 4 servings

This is another hit from our original menu. At the pace we run, we love putting things in the oven at night at 200 degrees F and waking up the next morning to find them beautifully cooked, falling apart, and ready to go. This is a subtly seasoned dish. It's inspired by Thai cooking, with ginger and lemongrass, and I think it's really important that your slaw is fresh. You want crisp cabbage and fresh cilantro so you can use them to their full potential. Have good soft buns on hand to serve with the pork.

1. Reheat the pork if it's been refrigerated. Split and butter the buns, and lightly toast them, cut side down, in a pan over medium heat. Spread about a table-spoon of aioli on the bottom of each bun, then top with about ¼ cup of slaw and about ⅓ cup of pork. Add the top buns and serve.

LEMONGRASS PORK

Makes 1 pound pork

1. Preheat oven to 200 degrees F.

2. Crush the lemongrass stalk with the side of a knife to help release its flavor. Trim the bottom and discard, then cut the stalk into 2-inch chunks. Set aside.

3. Thoroughly rub the curry paste, brown sugar, and salt all over the pork. Put the pork in a medium roasting pan. In a small mixing bowl, combine the lime juice and water and pour it over the pork. Scatter the gingerroot and lemongrass in the pan. Cover the pan tightly with aluminum foil and cook for 2 hours, or until the pork is falling apart. It should be tender enough to serve at this point, but break the meat up with a fork if you want smaller pieces. Season to taste with salt and pepper. Use immediately or allow the pork to cool, and refrigerate until ready to use. It will keep in the refrigerator 3 to 5 days, well wrapped.

1 stalk lemongrass

3 tablespoons red curry paste (available in Asian groceries or most well-stocked supermarkets)

5 teaspoons loosely packed dark brown sugar

5 teaspoons salt

1 pound pork butt

3 tablespoons lime juice (from 2 medium limes)

½ cup water or chicken stock

1 (3-inch) piece fresh gingerroot, peeled and sliced

Salt and freshly ground pepper

2 tablespoons soy sauce

1 green onion, finely chopped

1 tablespoon unseasoned rice vinegar

1½ teaspoons light brown sugar

2 garlic cloves, minced

1½ cups mayonnaise

1½ teaspoons peeled, finely chopped gingerroot

¼ cup chopped cilantro

¼ cup sweet chili sauce, such as Mae Ploy

½ lime, zested (about ½ teaspoon zest)

GINGER "AIOLI"

Makes about 2 cups

1. Mix all the ingredients in a large bowl. Refrigerate until ready to use. The aioli will keep for up to a week.

SPICY PICKLED CABBAGE SLAW

Makes about 3 cups

The kick in this dish comes from the touch of sambal oelek, *an Indonesian chili paste. If you can't find it, substitute* Sriracha, *a Thai chili sauce that's become popular in the U.S. in recent years and is stocked in most supermarkets. This dish makes enough for leftovers; use the slaw on sandwiches or as a spicy side to burgers.*

1. Put the cabbage and cilantro into a large bowl. In a small saucepan, bring the vinegar, water, salt, sugar, *sambal oelek*, gingerroot, and sesame oil to a boil. Boil for 10 minutes, then remove from the heat and pour the dressing over the cabbage and cilantro. Allow the slaw to cool, then refrigerate until ready to use. It will keep for up to 3 days.

½ head napa cabbage, cut into julienne strips

¼ cup chopped cilantro

½ cup white vinegar

½ cup water

¼ cup salt

¼ cup sugar

1 tablespoon *sambal oelek* or *Sriracha* sauce

2-inch piece fresh gingerroot, peeled and minced

½ teaspoon sesame oil

fried chicken sandwich with pickled jalapeño "aioli"

||||||||||||||||||||||||||||||||||||||||||||||||||||||||||||||||||||||||||||||||||||||||||||||||||||||||||||||||||||||||||||||||||||||||

Makes 4 sandwiches

This is one sandwich people either love or hate because there's so much fennel in it. I'm a fan of fennel seed, so it's pretty aggressively spiced. The key is to let the chicken sit after you bread it; give it a good 15 to 20 minutes at room temperature. This helps the breading adhere. Note: This is not a recipe to choose for a last-minute meal. The chicken needs to be brined overnight, and you'll need to make an advance batch of pickled jalapeños before you can use them in the aioli.

1. The night before you plan to make the sandwiches, put the chicken thighs in a large roasting pan. Cover them with the chicken brine, then cover the pan with plastic wrap and refrigerate.

2. When you're ready to fry the chicken, transfer the thighs from the brine to a large plate and coat them

4 (6-ounce) boneless, skinless chicken thighs

1 quart cold Chicken Brine (page 55)

3 cups Chicken Flour (page 56)

1½ quarts canola oil

4 potato-style rolls, split and toasted

1 cup Pickled Jalapeño "Aioli,", divided (page 57)

3 cups kale, cut into long, thin ribbons (chiffonade)

liberally with the chicken flour. Set them aside for at least 15 minutes.

3. In a large dutch oven or cast-iron skillet with deep sides, heat the canola oil over medium heat until it shimmers. Carefully add the chicken thighs, and fry until they reach an internal temperature of 162 degrees F when measured with an instant-read thermometer. Remove the thighs from the oil and set them aside on a roasting rack. (Set paper towels underneath the rack to catch drips for an easier cleanup.)

4. Spread each side of the rolls with a tablespoon of aioli. Lightly dress the kale with the remaining ½ cup aioli and divide it among the bottom buns. Add a piece of fried chicken on top of the kale, add the top bun, and take a big bite of deliciousness.

CHICKEN BRINE

Makes about 5 cups

1. Mix the sugar, salt, bay leaves, peppercorns, fennel seeds, and thyme in a large bowl. Pour the hot water over the mixture and let it steep for at least 30 minutes. Store in the refrigerator until ready to use. It will keep for up to a week.

2 tablespoons sugar

¼ cup salt

2 dried bay leaves

¼ cup peppercorns

¼ cup fennel seeds

¼ cup dried thyme

4 cups hot water

4 cups flour

1½ teaspoons freshly ground pepper

1 teaspoon garlic salt

1½ teaspoons dried ground sage

3 tablespoon fennel seeds

1½ teaspoons dried dill

1½ teaspoons celery seeds

1½ teaspoons smoked paprika

1½ teaspoons chile powder

1½ teaspoons sugar

1½ teaspoons salt

1½ teaspoons onion powder

1½ teaspoons crushed red pepper flakes

CHICKEN FLOUR

Makes about 4 cups

1. Mix all the ingredients in a large bowl and set aside.

PICKLED JALAPEÑO "AIOLI"

Makes about 2 cups

1. Mix all the ingredients together in a large bowl. Refrigerate until ready to use. The aioli will keep in the refrigerator for up to a week.

2 cups mayonnaise

3 Pickled Jalapeños, diced (page 58)

½ medium lemon, first zested, then juiced

1½ teaspoons minced garlic

½ teaspoon freshly ground pepper

1 tablespoon pickling juice from the jalapeños

15 jalapeños

2 cups red wine vinegar

1 cup red wine (cabernet or merlot)

2 cups water

1 cup sugar

6 dried bay leaves

1 tablespoon caraway seeds

1 tablespoon black peppercorns

1 tablespoon ground cumin

1 tablespoon ground coriander

1 tablespoon red pepper flakes

1 tablespoon chopped garlic

PICKLED JALAPEÑOS

Makes 15 peppers

1. Hold the jalapeños with tongs and char them in batches by holding them over a gas flame. If you don't have a gas stove, broil them on high heat, rotating them occasionally, about 6 to 8 minutes, until all sides are blackened. Transfer them to a bowl, cover it with plastic wrap or a towel, and allow them to soften and cool. When the jalapeños are cool enough to handle, peel and stem them. Then cut in half length-wise and remove the seeds. Put the charred jalapeños in a large bowl and set aside.

2. Mix the vinegar, wine, water, sugar, bay leaves, caraway seeds, peppercorns, cumin, coriander, red pepper flakes, and garlic in a large saucepan and bring to a boil. Remove the pickling juice from the heat and pour it over the jalapeños. Let them sit for at least 30 minutes before using. Reserve 1 tablespoons pickling juice to make the Pickled Jalapeño "Aioli" (page 57). Leftover jalapeños are great in other sandwiches and salads, or as garnish.

egg salad sandwich

Makes 4 sandwiches

This is our twist on the classic sandwich. It's open faced, and I think it's all about the egg. Eggs are a test for us cooks sometimes—if you can cook an egg, you can cook anything. This soft-cooked version is inspired by the Momofuku *cookbook from the New York restaurant. Momofuku chef David Chang calls it the "5.10" egg, for the time it takes to get the perfect balance of firm whites and soft yolk. When making the dish, remember this: the "sauce" binding the egg salad together is all about the yolk. Exact timing is what makes it work, so make sure you have a watch or timer handy when you cook the eggs.*

½ cup red onion, cut into thin half-moons

1 cup sherry vinegar

1 cup Crème Fraîche (page 26)

8 large eggs

4 slices brioche or soft white bread, toasted

1 small head frisée

1 teaspoon smoked paprika

A few pinches of flake sea salt

1. Start by quickly pickling the onions. Put the onions in a small bowl. Boil the sherry vinegar in a small saucepan, pour it over the onions, and let the mixture sit for 20 minutes. Pull the onions out and set them aside, reserving the vinegar. Use as much of the vinegar as you need in order to thin the crème fraîche

until it is loose enough to drizzle from a spoon, and set it aside.

2. Prepare an ice bath for the eggs by filling a large bowl with ice and water. Bring a large pot of water to a boil. Now, the precision part: place the eggs in the boiling water and wait 5 minutes and 10 seconds. Using a slotted spoon, transfer the eggs to the ice bath. Let them cool for 15 minutes, then pull them out and peel them gently under a trickle of water.

3. To assemble the sandwich, place the peeled eggs in a medium bowl of warm water. Let them sit for 5 minutes. Arrange the brioche on a serving plate. Using a slotted spoon, gently place 2 eggs on each slice. With a fork, slightly split the eggs right on the bread, letting some yolk out to get a head start on the "salad." Top the eggs with 3 or 4 frisée leaves and scatter a few pickled onion slices over the greens. Drizzle crème fraîche over the onions. Sprinkle with a little smoked paprika and finish each sandwich with a pinch of sea salt.

duck tacos

‖‖‖

Makes 4 servings

This is another of our most popular items. The idea for this recipe came out of doing a lot of catering events where we had some leftover duck legs, and we felt like we could do something more interesting than make them into confit. I like the richness of the duck in the tacos—it's saltier than pork and fattier than chicken. The preparation is really simple: we cure the legs overnight, which is basically adding salt and/or sugar to draw the excess water from the meat. Removing the water slows the bacterial growth and also gives the meat great flavor. Then we roast them until the meat falls off the bone. Once you've prepared the meat, the taco is a simple pleasure: fatty duck cut by sharp, clean flavors. Leave the skin on if you can—then you get the best part, the crispy bits. You'll have plenty of salsa left over for chips or to use later.

1. Pick the meat from the roasted duck legs and warm it gently in a large, lightly oiled pan over medium-low heat. Lightly char the tortillas over a gas flame, or

4 Roasted Duck Legs (page 62)

8 white corn tortillas

1 cup Smoky Salsa (page 63)

4 sprigs fresh cilantro, for garnish

¼ cup minced white onion

Hot sauce (such as Tapatío or Cholula), optional

warm them over low heat in a dry cast-iron skillet. Double up the tortillas, place about ½ cup of duck meat in the center of each, and top with a few teaspoons of salsa, a sprig of cilantro, and a few diced onions. Add a few drops of hot sauce if you like more kick.

---

4 cups loosely packed dark brown sugar

1 cup salt

2 tablespoons ground cumin

1 tablespoon ground cinnamon

1 tablespoon ground coriander

1 tablespoon freshly ground pepper

4 duck legs

ROASTED DUCK LEGS

Makes 4 legs

1. In a large mixing bowl, combine the brown sugar, salt, cumin, cinnamon, coriander, and pepper. In a roasting pan or other deep pan, cover the duck legs completely with a liberal amount of the cure mix. Cover and refrigerate overnight.

2. When you're ready to roast the duck, preheat the oven to 330 degrees F. Brush the cure off the legs, and place the legs on a baking sheet that has a little water in the bottom. Roast for about 1½ hours, or until the meat is falling apart. Set aside to cool.

SMOKY SALSA

Makes 5 cups

1. Heat the oil over medium-low heat in a large skillet. Cook the onion, chipotle, and garlic for about 5 minutes, until they are soft but not browned. Reduce the heat to low, add the tomatoes with their juices, sugar, salt, and pepper, and simmer for 10 minutes.

2. Char the tortillas over a gas burner until there is very little white left, only about 20 percent. (Alternatively, toast them in a dry skillet, but don't be afraid of a little smoke—you really want them blackened.) Add the whole charred tortillas to the tomato mixture and remove it from the heat. Add the cilantro and lime zest and juice, then purée the salsa and tortillas using an immersion blender. (A food processor or regular blender will work too.) Taste the seasonings and adjust if necessary.

1 tablespoon olive oil

½ medium white onion, sliced

1 canned chipotle chile

2 cloves garlic

4 cups (about 32 ounces) canned whole peeled tomatoes, with juice,

1 tablespoon sugar

1 tablespoon salt

½ tablespoon freshly ground pepper

2 white corn tortillas

¼ cup chopped cilantro

1 medium lime, first zested, then juiced

chicken salad

4 cups cubed roasted chicken breast

1 cup finely chopped celery

¼ cup minced capers

¼ cup minced cornichons

1 tablespoon cornichon juice

¼ cup chopped fresh dill

¼ cup whole fresh tarragon leaves

½ medium shallot, minced

2 cloves garlic, minced

½ cup mayonnaise

1 tablespoon sweet hot mustard

Juice of ½ medium lemon (about 1½ tablespoons)

1 tablespoon salt

½ tablespoon freshly ground pepper

Makes enough salad for 4 sandwiches

We took the classic chicken salad ratios and made a few basic but delicious additions: cornichons (a sour French gherkin) and hot mustard. Most chicken salad recipes are centered on the herbs, and while dill and tarragon are still essential ingredients in our recipe, the mustard adds kick and the pickles perk it up.

You can buy a pre-roasted chicken, but I think the key to a good chicken salad is perfectly cooked chicken, and that usually means doing it yourself. The only way to do this is not to overcook the chicken. And what does that mean? It means not cooking it to 185 degrees F. Pull the chicken out when its internal temperature reaches 160 degrees F and let it rest. Please, if you do one thing when preparing chicken, do this. You don't want to be known as the person who always cooked chicken so dry it tasted like sandpaper.

I guarantee that every other chicken salad recipe will taste two-dimensional after you prepare this 1-2-3 flavor punch. To serve, just pile the salad on toasted slices of artisan-style honey wheat bread and top with 2 slices of tomato and a handful of greens. Shazam! You now have a fresh, herby, substantial sandwich.

1. Mix all the ingredients in a large bowl. Refrigerate if not using immediately. The chicken salad will keep in the refrigerator for up to 3 days.

skillet poutine

Makes 4 servings

First of all, this is not classic Canadian poutine, which uses cheese curds. This is America—we did it our way. I tried it first with curds, but they have more squeak than flavor, kind of like the Canadians when they bitch about our poutine. The other difference is that we mix all the yumminess together instead of piling it up on top of the fries—there's better distribution that way. Note: You need to start this dish the night before you expect to serve it; the fries take time to prepare.

1 to 2 cups Poutine Gravy (page 68)

1 batch Skillet Fries (page 70)

1 cup grated sharp cheddar cheese

1 cup grated Grana Padano or Parmigiano-Reggiano cheese

½ cup mixed chopped fresh dill, Italian parsley, and sage

Salt and freshly ground pepper

1. Reheat 1 to 2 cups of gravy, depending on how saucy you want your poutine. Using tongs, transfer a freshly cooked batch of Skillet fries to a large bowl and add the gravy, cheeses, and herbs. Lightly toss, taking care not to break up the fries. Season to taste with salt and pepper. Distribute evenly among 4 plates or bowls.

¼ cup (½ stick) butter

½ cup diced yellow onion

2 tablespoons diced carrot

2 tablespoons diced celery

⅓ teaspoon tomato paste

¼ cup all-purpose flour

2¾ cups beef stock

½ tablespoon Worcestershire sauce

⅜ teaspoon chopped fresh garlic

⅜ teaspoon salt

⅜ teaspoon freshly ground pepper

2 tablespoons chopped fresh sage

2 tablespoons chopped fresh rosemary

POUTINE GRAVY

Makes about 3 cups

I think if you're going to do a gravy for anything, you need to make it from scratch. A dish like this relies on the flavors and textures you get from taking the time to put together a real gravy, not thickening it with cornstarch. You can freeze any extra poutine gravy, but why not use it for other purposes instead? People put it on everything—try it over rice, mashed potatoes, meatloaf, roast turkey, or wherever you can use a sauce rich with herbs and butter and beef.

1. In a large dutch oven or stockpot, melt the butter over medium-high heat. Cook the onion, carrot, and celery until they're well caramelized, colored good and brown. Add the tomato paste, then the flour, and sauté them together for a minute or two, making a sort of roux. Add the beef stock, Worcestershire, and garlic, and simmer for 35 minutes. Add the salt, pepper, sage, and rosemary, and simmer for an additional 10 minutes. Purée the gravy with an immersion blender (a food processor or blender will also work). Taste the seasonings and adjust if necessary.

4 large russet potatoes

2 quarts canola oil

SKILLET FRIES

Makes 4 servings

We love these fries in poutine, but we also serve them with aiolis and dips (see page 72). It takes some extra time to do fries right. The key to a great fry is 100 percent about soaking them in advance to wash away the extra starch and then frying them twice—once at 300 degrees F and again at 350 degrees F when you're ready to eat them.

1. Wash the potatoes and cut them, with the peels still on, into fries about ¼ inch thick. Soak them overnight in a large bowl of water. The next morning, drain them well in a colander, then spread them on a cloth or paper towel–lined pan. Allow them to fully dry. You don't want any moisture on them, lest you spatter hot oil when you start to fry them.

2. Preheat the canola oil in a large dutch oven to 300 degrees F, as measured by a deep-fry thermometer. Using a slotted spoon, transfer the fries to the oil. If you fry them in batches, make sure the oil comes back up to temperature between batches. Fry them for 8 to 10 minutes, or until they're lightly golden.

Remove them with a slotted spoon and lay them out on a sheet tray to dry. (They're actually even better if you refrigerate them for a day or two at this step, but that's not absolutely necessary. If you want to prep extra batches and freeze them, this is the point to put them in the freezer.)

3. When the fries are dry and you're ready to serve them, heat the oil in the dutch oven again, this time to 350 degrees F. Using a slotted spoon, transfer the fries to the oil and fry for 3 to 5 minutes, or until they're golden brown.

"aiolis"

These are not true aiolis, which are made by emulsifying oil, egg yolks, and garlic, but our fancy word for our fancy mayonnaises. Pairing these dips with french fries takes you to a whole new condiment level: simple mayo is fine (and very French), and ketchup is classic, but these pack a flavorful punch. Once you get the hang of mixing and matching the ingredients, play with other combinations. Chiles make great aioli flavorings, especially chipotles. We use the following dips with our Skillet Fries (page 70), but they're also great to spice up sandwiches and tacos. They'll keep in the refrigerator for up to a week.

2 or 3 bulbs garlic

½ cup olive oil

2 tablespoons salt

½ tablespoon freshly ground pepper

3 cups mayonnaise

¼ cup apple cider vinegar

GARLIC "AIOLI"

Makes about 3 cups

1. Preheat the oven to 325 degrees F. Place the garlic bulbs on a layer of aluminum foil and drizzle them liberally with the olive oil, maybe 2 tablespoons for each head, plus a pinch of the salt and pepper. Wrap tightly in the foil and bake until soft, about 1 hour. Allow the

bulbs to cool, then squeeze the soft garlic from the papery cloves into a large bowl. Add the mayonnaise, remaining salt and pepper, and apple cider vinegar, and combine. Refrigerate until ready to use.

HERB "AIOLI"

Makes about 2½ cups

1. Mix all the ingredients in a large bowl. Refrigerate until ready to use.

2 cups mayonnaise

1 tablespoon stemmed fresh thyme leaves

1 tablespoon chopped fresh sage leaves

1 tablespoon chopped fresh tarragon leaves

1 tablespoon chopped fresh rosemary leaves

Juice of 1 medium lemon (about 3 tablespoons)

¼ cup cider vinegar

¾ teaspoon freshly ground pepper

4 teaspoons salt

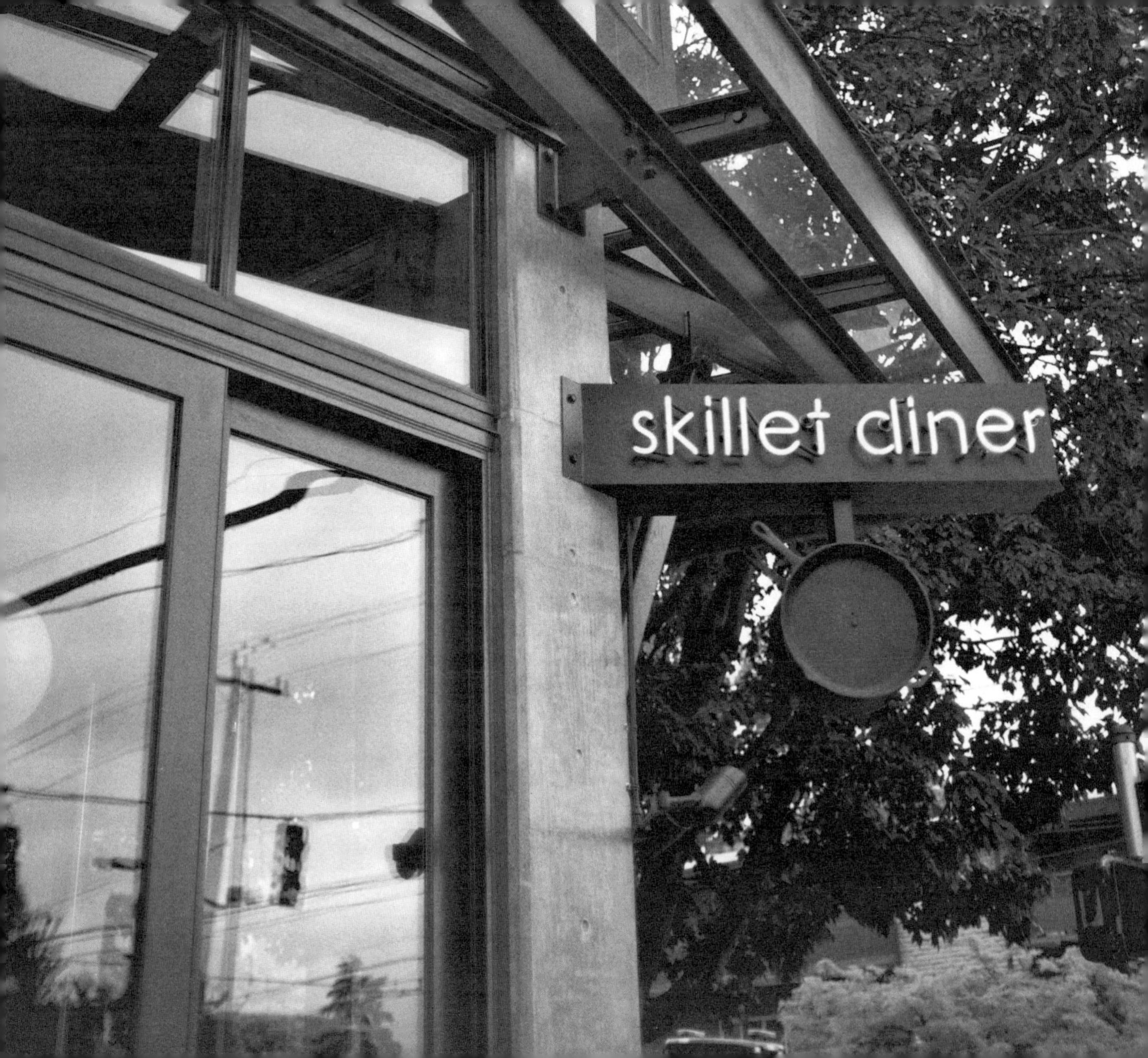
skillet diner

The Diner

I got out of restaurants because I was tired of doing the same old thing all the time. So how did I wind up opening a sit-down Skillet Diner in one of Seattle's coolest, most walkable neighborhoods?

I guess it's because in this case, I could create what I wanted—and have the freedom to not have to work at it every day myself.

I also thought our customers deserved this kind of place. America has a real dearth of midrange restaurants. They're all either fine dining or crap. But a neighborhood joint to go get some pancakes or honest food done well, in a nice environment? That's pretty rare. Building one would also give the business more stability, a place where customers could always find us and eat comfortably, even when the rain was coming down. This being Seattle, that covers a lot of days.

The food is definitely hit-you-in-the-face. It's not finessed; we're not talking subtlety here, and that's fine. That's what a diner should be—at least, this particular one. It's relaxed and fun and high quality. We're capturing the spirit of what we do on wheels, but the fixed space gives us its own kind of freedom. It really expands the menu, because on the trailer, you're limited to a grill, fryer, or four burners, and the burners get very limited use because of speed. There's a ton of stuff we get to do at the diner that we can't do on the truck.

The first cups of coffee and orders of Leavened Cornmeal Waffle with Braised Pork Belly and Sunny-Side Egg (page 11) come in when we open at 7 a.m., and on our late nights the orders of Nutella Crostini (page 128) roll out until 2 a.m. The Fried Chicken Sandwich (page 53) is the early favorite and the one our executive chef and general manager, Brian O'Connor, recommends for those new to Skillet.

I didn't want this to be a kitsch, retro, clichéd diner. I wanted us to use natural ingredients and for our customers to feel some warmth when they walked in. I didn't want it all Formica and stainless steel. At the same time, a diner needs to be functional—that's why they're made with Formica and stainless steel. But there were a couple of attributes of the classic diner that we did definitely want. A counter with stools was one, and booths, and being able to look across the whole restaurant with open sightlines. We gave our customers gift certificates in exchange for old skillets to decorate our wall, and the booths are a color that one writer called "1979 Frigidaire green."

I have to say, a restaurant is easier to manage than a street-food cart. There are so many fewer moving parts. At a diner you kind of know what's going to be hard. It's always going to be employees that are a challenge, managing your costs—it's all pretty predictable. One day our Internet was down, but we muddled through. But with street food, when a tire goes flat or a propane hose goes, it's a different animal.

The diner was a fast hit. We had hour-long waits for a table right after we opened. If you have to have a problem, that's a good one to have. Now I'm thinking of other ways we could fit our spirit inside four walls. Maybe a beer hall? Something simple with grilled meats, pickled vegetables, crusty breads, a ton of beers, and great service with some warmth. A lot of places in town have tons of great beers, but they miss the boat on the food. I think people underrate service sometimes. I think it has to be a massive aspect of whatever you're doing. Whatever other projects we take on, it'll always be big for us.

dinner

Salad Vinaigrettes

Kale Caesar Salad

Skillet Burger

Chanterelle Risotto

Semolina Pasta

Quick To-Go Pasta

Folded Lasagna

Mac 'n' Cheese

Farro Burger

Sockeye with Mashed Potatoes

INITIALLY, SKILLET didn't do dinner. People go home to eat with their families after work; they don't generally grab a bite on the street. And, as I said earlier, working more than one meal dragged the shifts out too long. But after a few months of serving lunch, we started getting calls from our daily customers asking if we would cater their wedding, and then calls from companies wondering whether we'd pull the truck up to their office Christmas party. We added employees, and now dinner is a regular part of Skillet life: at catering events, at the diner, and in front of stadiums.

When we serve lunch at the trailer, we're serving one person at a time, but with dinner and events and the diner, we're serving a group of people sharing a moment. I love being able to facilitate events and dinners in unusual places. We've driven the trailer everywhere from San Juan Island beaches to Eastern Washington's rolling hills. We've done everything from serving poutine to a bunch of Cirque du Soleil clowns to cooking on a Weber grill on a sidewalk in downtown Seattle. To me, that's the most exciting way to cook dinner: in an environment where people are focused on what's happening across from them in conversation, and the medium is the food being passed in front of them.

salad vinaigrettes

Salads can be very boring. We add some excitement by using different great, locally produced greens and lots of herbs. I think more people would enjoy salads if they tried greens like red oak, arugula, kale, chard, and baby romaine. The difference between using a mass-produced head of lettuce and one that's grown from soil in your backyard is mind-blowing. Taste-test a head of romaine from a local farm next to one from the grocery store, and you'll probably say, "Wow, that's what romaine is supposed to taste like." I also believe that herbs should be used like greens. We use Italian parsley and basil right alongside traditional salad greens. Top your mixed greens with either of these vibrant vinaigrettes. I also think the key to salad is focusing on knife skills—there are some salads that need to be chopped up small and others that don't. It really depends on how you want each bit to translate. Basically, salads deserve to be thought through.

RED WINE VINAIGRETTE

Makes about 4½ cups

1. Add all the ingredients to a large container, cover, and shake vigorously until well combined.

- 1¾ cups red wine vinegar
- 1 tablespoon minced shallots
- 2¼ cups canola oil
- 1 tablespoon salt
- 1 teaspoon freshly ground pepper
- 1 tablespoon dried thyme
- ¼ cup red wine, preferably Chianti or merlot

HERB VINAIGRETTE

Makes about 3½ cups

1. Add all the ingredients to a large container, cover, and shake vigorously until well combined.

- 1½ cups champagne vinegar
- 1¾ cups olive oil
- 1 tablespoon chopped fresh basil
- 1 tablespoon chopped fresh sage
- 1 tablespoon fresh thyme
- 1 tablespoon chopped fresh tarragon
- 1 tablespoon chopped fresh rosemary
- 1 tablespoon salt
- 1½ teaspoons freshly ground pepper
- 1 tablespoon minced garlic

kale caesar salad

FOR THE CROUTONS:

4 cups day-old bread cut into 1-inch cubes

3 tablespoons olive oil

1 teaspoon freshly ground pepper

1 teaspoon salt

FOR THE CAESAR DRESSING:

2 small cloves garlic, minced

¼ teaspoon salt

1 teaspoon anchovy paste

1 teaspoon lemon zest

2 tablespoons freshly squeezed lemon juice

1 teaspoon Dijon-style mustard

1 teaspoon Worcestershire sauce

1 cup mayonnaise

Makes 4 servings

My buddy Cormac Mahoney inspired this salad. He has a kale salad on the menu at his restaurant in Seattle, Madison Park Conservatory. He taught me that using raw kale is OK. Most kale recipes call for cooking it down into a mush, robbing it of its dense texture and strong, wholesome taste. Cormac freed me from that. I played around with a few dressings and discovered that kale and Caesar are a match made in heaven. Most other greens can't stand up to the rich and creamy Caesar dressing, but the kale just shines through. In turn the dressing helps quiet the bitter kale taste, which can be too strong on its own. This salad tastes healthy and hearty at the same time. To top the salad, we like to use boquerónes, *little Spanish anchovies that are packed in vinegar. You can find them in the deli section of well-stocked markets and specialty shops. If you can't find them, plain anchovies work fine too.*

1. To prepare the croutons, preheat the oven to 350 degrees F. In a large bowl, toss the bread cubes

with the olive oil, pepper, and salt until well coated. Spread the bread cubes in a single layer on a baking sheet and bake for 10 minutes, or until they're golden brown. Allow them to cool and set aside.

2. To prepare the Caesar dressing, in a large bowl mash the garlic cloves into a paste with the salt. Add the anchovy paste, lemon zest and juice, mustard, Worcestershire, mayonnaise, parmesan, and pepper and combine.

3. To assemble the salad, toss the kale with 1 cup of the dressing. Divide the salad among 4 plates, piling it so it stands tall. Scatter croutons over the top and criss-cross 2 *boquerónes* in an X on the top of each plate.

½ **cup freshly grated parmesan cheese**

1 **tablespoon coarsely ground pepper**

FOR THE SALAD:

1 **pound lacinato (aka dinosaur) kale, stems and center ribs discarded and leaves cut into long, thin ribbons (chiffonade)**

8 *boquerónes* **or plain anchovy fillets**

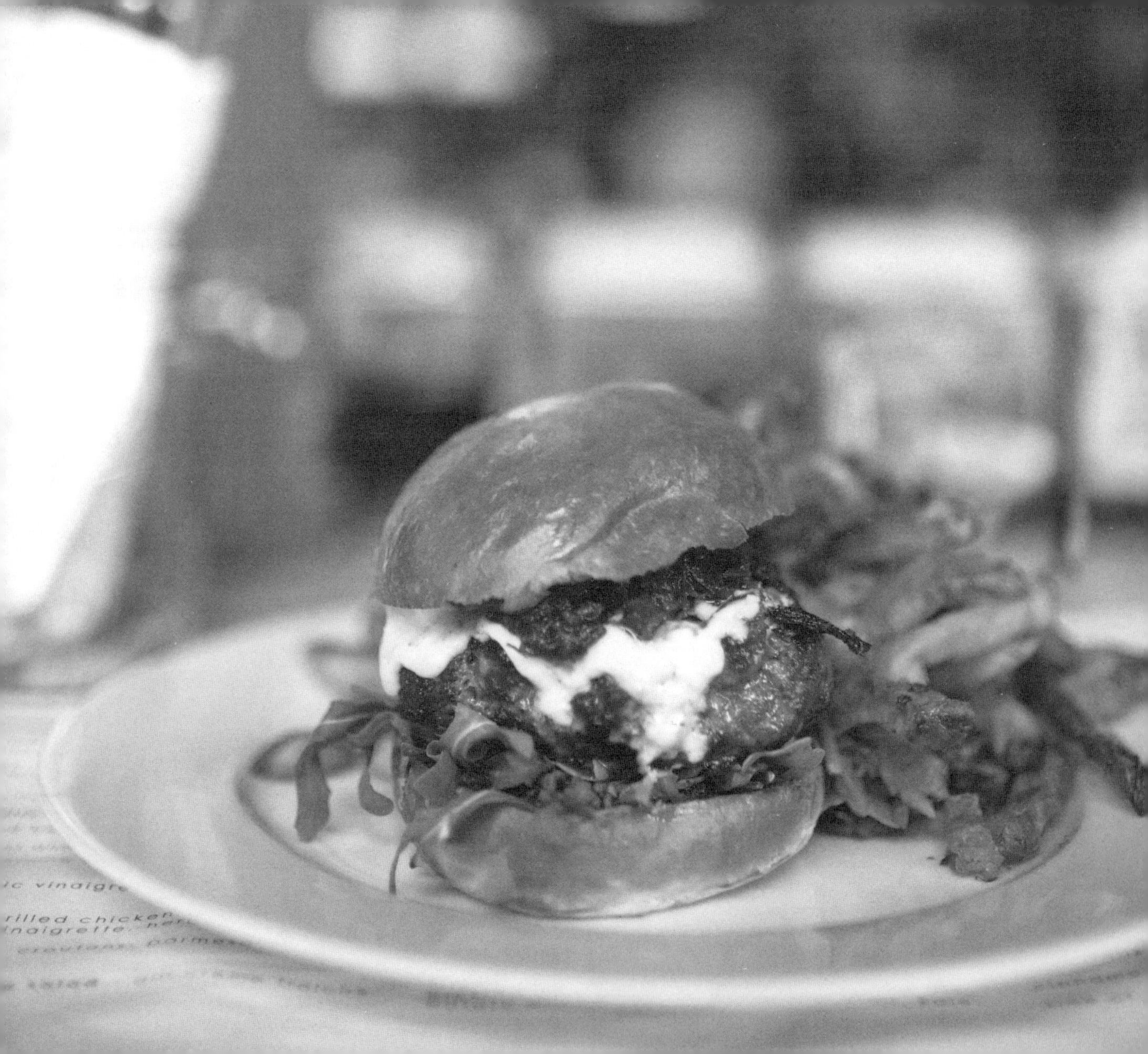

skillet burger

Makes 4 burgers

Our burger is inspired by the one at Father's Office in Santa Monica. I lived there for three years and would eat that burger at least once a week. This burger has made us who we are, in a sense—it's a great marriage of complementary flavors, with the saltiness of blue cheese, the bitterness of arugula, the sweetness of bacon jam, and the solid foundation of the bun. It's consistently been the most ordered item on the menu at the cart and the diner. It's been on magazine covers, featured on TV—it's basically our opus.

4 (6-ounce) patties high-quality ground beef, grass-fed if possible

Salt and freshly ground pepper

4 brioche buns, split

4 (1-ounce) slices Cambozola cheese

8 tablespoons Skillet Bacon Jam (see page 91 for mail-order details) or another bacon jam or strips of cooked bacon

2 cups loosely packed arugula

1. Season the patties well with salt and pepper. Preheat an outdoor gas grill or heat a stovetop grill pan on medium. When the grill is hot, quickly toast the buns, and set them aside. Grill the burgers for about 3 minutes on one side. Flip them, place the cheese on top, and cook for about 3 minutes on the second side.

Remove the burgers from the heat and let them rest for another 3 minutes. Spread each side of the buns with a tablespoon of bacon jam. Pile some arugula on the bottom buns and add the burgers.

Bacon Jam

Our bacon jam is just bacon and onions caramelized with balsamic vinegar, brown sugar, salt, and pepper. That's it. Six ingredients. It's super simple.

I first started using it for some of my catering events. Then when we started Skillet, I decided to use it on our burger. Bacon and beef were pretty much meant to be together, and the jam is sort of the ketchup of our burger; it has the sweet tanginess you need to balance out the char of the meat and the salty blue cheese and arugula.

From the beginning, people started asking for more of it. They just kept requesting it. I didn't really want to sell it retail on the trailer. I was busy enough just trying to keep up with this crazy street-food business. But then I thought, "Wait a second. This is one thing we could do on a larger scale and expand." If we did twelve trailers, I couldn't see us having the same quality on each one; there are way too many moving parts. But bacon jam, produced in one facility—you can control that process. So we started selling it by the jar.

It's a good thing we did, because it wound up saving our business.

In late 2008 we were close to shutting down. We were giving ourselves until January. It came down to the fact that I wasn't getting paid. Every week it was, "Am I getting a paycheck? Will we be able to pay our bills?" I believed in Skillet 100 percent, but you can only go on for so long when you're killing your-self financially. Then the Christmas season came. Martha Stewart listed us in her gift guide; it was on her website's front page. *Real Simple* magazine did the same. The next thing I knew, we had $150,000 in orders. Instead of prepar-ing for our last days, we were hiring as many people as we could find. My dad came and helped. Huck, our little boy, had just been born. I was carrying him on my chest in a sling and making jam. It was a little bit overwhelming—I kept thinking the orders were going to stop, but they didn't.

Maybe I resisted the jam at first, but at that point, you really can't not be on board. Now we sell the jam online and through specialty shops and at our diner. We've had customers use it for bacon jam grilled cheese and crostini, bacon jam hand-pies, bacon jam–stuffed pork chops. . . . If you Googled "bacon jam" in 2007, you only had maybe ten mentions. Today there are at least a mil-lion. I like to think we had some part in a phenomenon.

The only downside to that kind of success is the fight it takes to keep what made it special in the first place. Anytime you start doing something on a large scale, you'll run into the notion that you should make it cheaper, you should make it faster. In manufactur-ing, that's what it's all about. When you start getting food involved, the indus-try wants to stabilize it, and that usu-ally means including something that's not natural. We're very close to making a shelf-stable jam, but that's through experiments like increasing the vinegar content. It would be very easy for us to make a corn syrup–based bacon jam that looked amazing from the minute it came in the jar, unrefrigerated, to six months later when you opened it up in the pantry. But I have zero interest—less than zero interest—in doing that. We're going to keep it the same way.

ORDER ONLINE AT
SkilletStreetFood.com/BaconJam

chanterelle risotto

½ cup extra-virgin olive oil, divided

½ cup (1 stick) unsalted butter, divided

2 medium shallots, minced

2 cups crisp white wine, divided

1 fresh bay leaf

Leaves from 3 sprigs fresh thyme

2 cups carnaroli or arborio rice

6 cups beef or veal stock

¾ pound fresh chanterelle mushrooms, cleaned and pulled apart

Sea salt and freshly ground pepper

1 cup freshly grated parmesan cheese

½ cup chopped Italian parsley

Makes 8 servings

Most people were shocked to see a risotto on our food truck. That was one of the times where people were like, "Huh? This is coming out of the food trailer?!" We're not an Italian restaurant, we're a food truck, so we're doing it the best we can, not with complete technical authenticity. It's important to keep it simple: risotto and mushrooms and cracked pepper and lemon zest—you don't need much more than that.

A lot of people cook mushrooms before they put them in something, and that makes them flaccid. Instead of cutting the mushrooms, I pull them apart into pieces and let them go where they'd naturally go, and I don't cook them— they just go into the warm risotto and the risotto cooks them, so you get as much of the mushroom texture as possible. Wild mushrooms are a pretty prominent ingredient here in Washington, and I think they should be honored and showcased on their own. If you're feeling extra luxurious, garnish the risotto at the end with slices of white truffle. That's what we call super street fare.

1. Heat a large, wide, heavy-bottomed pan over medium-low heat. Add 2 tablespoons of the olive oil and 2 tablespoons of the butter and melt them together in the pan. Add the shallots and cook for 2 minutes, or until they're translucent. Pour 1 cup of the wine into the pan, add the bay leaf and thyme, and bring the liquid to a simmer, allowing the wine to evaporate, about 5 minutes. Discard the bay leaf.

2. Reduce the heat to low, and melt the remaining 6 tablespoons each of butter and oil in the pan. Stir in the rice and coat with the oil until the kernels are shiny, 3 to 5 minutes.

3. Add the stock one ladleful at a time, allowing the rice to absorb the liquid between additions. Do not add the stock too quickly, as it will affect the texture of the kernels. Stir the rice every 30 to 60 seconds, just to make sure it isn't sticking, over low heat until each ladle of the liquid is absorbed. (Don't stir it continuously unless you want oatmeal.) Repeat until most of the stock is incorporated and the rice is al dente—cooked but with a little bite to it—about 25 minutes. Fold the mushrooms into the rice and season to taste with salt and pepper. Remove the risotto from the heat. Stir in the parmesan and parsley and serve immediately.

semolina pasta

|||||||||||||||||||||||||||||||||||||||||||||||||||||||||||||||||||||||||||||||||||||||||||||||||||||||||||||||||||||||||||||||||||||||||

1½ cups (about 9 ounces) fine semolina flour

2 cups (about 9 ounces) "00" flour, or substitute all-purpose flour

5 medium eggs

Makes 4 servings

There's something about fresh pasta that dry pasta just can't replicate. The fresh version is so toothsome; it has such a different mouthfeel. There are dishes where dried pasta is best, but for the most part, fresh pasta really is the way to go, and it's easy to make with a pasta machine. We use a mixture of flours to create some texture in our pasta, as the semolina flour alone is a bit dense. "00" flour is ground super-fine, making for a smoother, more delicate pasta with lots of finesse. If you can't find these flours at a well-stocked grocery store, you can order them online from sites like KingArthurFlour.com. Serve this one with Skillet Meat Sauce (page 101) or use it in Quick To-Go Pasta (page 97).

1. In the bowl of a food processor, add the flour and eggs and pulse until the dough just forms a ball. Remove the ball and knead it briefly until the dough is consistently mixed and you've picked up all the crumbly bits. It shouldn't be very sticky—if it is, add more "00"

flour while kneading. At this point, you can refrigerate the dough for up to 2 days or use it immediately. If you refrigerate it, let it warm back up to room temperature before using; otherwise, it will be too stiff to work with.

2. When you're ready to use the dough, set the pasta maker on its thickest setting. Tear off a chunk of dough slightly larger than a golf ball and flatten it into a disc with your hands. Feed it through the machine three or four times, folding it over on itself after each pass. Toss a bit of "00" flour on the dough if it gets sticky. Repeat until you've used all the dough. You will have 5 to 7 small, flattened discs when finished.

3. Set the machine to an intermediate setting and pass all your discs through once more. Then go to the final setting (whatever your pasta maker recommends for fettuccine or spaghetti or whatever type of noodle you're making) and pass the discs through again. You may need to cut them in half if they're getting too long. I usually like mine to be 8 to 10 inches long.

4. If you'll be cooking your noodles right away, bring a large pot of water to a boil.

5. Cut the noodles. Make sure the dough is well floured so they don't stick. I usually cut about half of the batch, add them to the pot, and then add each subsequent batch to the pot as it comes off the cutter. This should go very quickly. I haven't noticed the small difference in cooking time between the first half and the rest having a real effect on the texture.

6. If you won't be cooking the pasta right away, then take each batch off the cutter, fluff it with a little more "00" flour, and place it on a baking sheet or in a resealable plastic bag. You can either refrigerate it to use the next day, or freeze it and use it whenever.

quick to-go pasta

Makes 3 to 4 servings

Pasta was the main course of my childhood. I love that this quick pasta is about just that: noodles. If you want to add more ingredients, this recipe's the perfect foundation for playing with flavors. Shellfish, game, or cured meats are all great ways to dress it up. We call for wild arugula here, which has a more intense flavor than the baby leaves that come prewashed in sealed bags. Odds are that any full-size arugula you buy in bunches will fit the bill.

1. Salt a pot of water until it tastes like the ocean and bring it to a boil. Cook the pappardelle until it is al dente. Drain the pasta in a colander, reserving ½ cup pasta water in a separate container.

2. Return the drained pasta to the pot. In a medium bowl, whisk together the lemon zest and juice, ¾ cup of the olive oil, Grana Padano, and red pepper flakes. Season to taste with salt and pepper. Pour the sauce

12 ounces pappardelle or Semolina Pasta (page 94)

1 teaspoon lemon zest

1 tablespoon freshly squeezed lemon juice

1 cup olive oil, divided

1½ cups freshly grated Grana Padano cheese, plus extra for garnish

1 tablespoon crushed red pepper flakes

Salt and freshly ground pepper

2 cups wild arugula

over the pasta and toss gently to combine. If the sauce needs thinning, add a bit of the reserved pasta water. Mix in the arugula. Divide the pasta among the plates, sprinkle with extra cheese, and drizzle with the remaining ¼ cup olive oil.

folded lasagna

Makes 4 servings

This is a quick lasagna. Yes, there is such a thing. Lasagna is typically an investment of time and money, and nothing beats fresh-made pasta to make it work. But you can buy fresh pasta sheets instead of making them, and you can fold them over the contents instead of taking time to arrange deeply layered noodles, which also lets you bake the dish quickly. On the trailer, we had to learn to adapt the favorites we wanted to serve, to get all the components we like from a dish and deconstruct them in a way—not like molecular gastronomy spheres and foams, but just presenting them in a new way, creating the tastes we wanted within the limitations we had. This lasagna is good for a family meal—it's something I make at home myself, even when I've got the time and equipment for other versions.

1. Preheat the oven to 400 degrees F. Oil a baking sheet.

2. Salt a large pot of water until it tastes like the ocean and bring it to a boil. Take a fresh sheet of pasta and cook it for about 3 minutes, or until al dente. Pull it

4 (6-by-6-inch) fresh pasta sheets

Good-quality extra-virgin olive oil, for oiling the baking sheet and for drizzling

2 cups ricotta cheese

1 cup mixed loosely packed fresh basil and oregano leaves

1 cup grated Pecorino Romano cheese, plus extra for garnish

Salt and freshly ground pepper

2 cups Skillet Meat Sauce (page 101)

About 16 wild mushrooms (we like to mix chanterelles and hedgehogs, but even shiitakes will work)

1 pound fresh mozzarella cheese, sliced into twelve ½-inch rounds

½ teaspoon crushed red pepper flakes

out, lay it on a cutting board, and drizzle it with a little olive oil. Spread it out on the baking sheet.

3. Add fillings to just one half of the sheet, as if you're making an omelet. First, dollop on some ricotta. Then scatter some basil and oregano leaves and Pecorino over the ricotta, and season to taste with salt and pepper. Spoon about 2 tablespoons of meat sauce over this, and place about 4 good-size mushrooms on the sauce. Cover the mushroom layer with another few tablespoons of sauce, then shingle 3 slices of mozzarella over the top. Fold the other side of the pasta sheet over the fillings, and lightly drizzle the top with olive oil. Repeat the process with the remaining 3 pasta sheets.

4. Bake the lasagna for about 15 minutes, or until the edges are slightly golden brown. Sprinkle a little Pecorino and a pinch of red pepper flakes over the top, and drizzle a little more olive oil on before serving.

SKILLET MEAT SAUCE

Makes about 5 cups

1. In a large dutch oven or other large, heavy-bottomed pot cook the sausage and pork over medium heat until caramelized and brown, and the meat has rendered its fat, 3 to 5 minutes each side. Remove from the pot and set aside. Add the onion, garlic, carrot, and fennel seeds, and cook until the vegetables have caramelized, 5 to 7 minutes. Deglaze the pan with the red wine, pouring it into the pan and stirring and scraping off the browned bits at the bottom with a wooden spoon. Add the tomatoes, mushrooms, red pepper flakes, balsamic vinegar, and sugar, add the meat back to the pan, and simmer over low heat for at least 2 hours, or until the meat is falling-apart tender. (Up to 4 hours is even better.)

2. Mix in the fresh herbs. Buzz the sauce lightly with an immersion blender or mix with a wooden spoon, and season to taste with salt and pepper.

6 ounces spicy Italian pork sausage

¼ pound pork shoulder, cut into chunks

¼ medium yellow onion, chopped

2 cloves garlic, chopped

¼ large carrot, peeled and cut into large chunks

½ teaspoon fennel seeds

¼ cup red wine, a classic like Chianti or whatever you would drink with dinner

24 ounces whole peeled canned tomatoes

¾ cup halved mushrooms

¼ teaspoon crushed red pepper flakes

1½ teaspoons balsamic vinegar

¾ teaspoon sugar

2 tablespoons each mixed fresh sage, rosemary, and basil leaves

Salt and freshly ground pepper

mac 'n' cheese

Makes 4 servings

Mac 'n' cheese is the quintessential American dish. I believe the keys to making it are correctly salting the water for your pasta and making a béchamel/cheese sauce correctly—from there you can take it wherever.

For the béchamel, the biggest thing is making sure you don't burn it. Watch it: you've got to commit to it and be there. If you don't, the minute you walk away is going to be the minute you burn it, and you're done. For salt, I was always told the water should taste like the ocean, and I think that's pretty straightforward. People tend to use less than they think—I know I do. You have to taste the water. If you don't salt your water at the start, you're cutting your leg off. No matter what you do down the line, you're not going to get the full base of flavor you should. It's one of the things that drives me nuts with cooks. I'll taste the pasta and say, "Are you kidding me? You didn't salt the water!" You don't have to tell me. I know.

½ cup (1 stick) butter

½ cup all-purpose flour

1 tablespoon olive oil

½ medium yellow onion, sliced

2 cups whole milk

2 cups heavy cream

A few pinches of freshly grated nutmeg

Freshly ground pepper

¼ pound Grana Padano cheese, grated

¼ pound cheddar cheese, shredded

¼ pound provolone cheese, shredded

1 tablespoon salt

4 cups cooked penne or orecchiette or other small pasta

continued

1 cup fresh or thawed frozen peas

½ cup Guanciale (page 29) cut into julienne strips

5 fresh sage leaves, cut into thin ribbons (chiffonade)

1 cup Black Pepper Bread Crumbs (page 105)

1. Start by making the béchamel. Melt the butter in a small saucepan over medium-low heat. Whisk in the flour and stir for 1 minute, until the flour loses its raw flavor and the mixture forms a thick paste. This is your roux. Take it off the heat and set aside. In a large skillet, heat the olive oil. Add the onions and cook them over medium heat for a few minutes, until they're translucent. Mix in the roux and warm it for about 1 minute, just until it's heated through. Add the milk, cream, a pinch of nutmeg, and a teaspoon of pepper. Bring the sauce to a simmer, constantly stirring and checking to make sure it doesn't burn—believe me on this one, you gotta watch it. When the sauce has come together and thickened enough to coat the back of a spoon, about 15 minutes, turn off the heat and add all the cheeses and the salt. Buzz with an immersion blender or whisk together until the sauce is smooth and the cheese is thoroughly combined. Set aside.

2. Preheat the oven to 400 degrees F. Pour a cup of the béchamel sauce into a medium pan and bring it to a simmer over medium heat. Add the precooked pasta and cook until heated through. Add the peas,

guanciale, another pinch of nutmeg, and sage. Taste
and adjust the seasonings if necessary.

3. Divide the mac 'n' cheese among 4 small cast-iron
   skillets or baking dishes. Top each with ¼ cup of black
   pepper bread crumbs and a sprinkle of nutmeg. Bake
   for 10 minutes, or until the bread crumbs turn a deep
   golden brown. Cool to just above room temperature
   before serving.

BLACK PEPPER BREAD CRUMBS

Makes 1 cup

¼ cup (½ stick) butter

1 tablespoon freshly ground
pepper

¾ teaspoon salt

1 cup soft bread crumbs

1. Melt the butter in a large skillet over medium heat.
   Stir in the pepper and salt. Toast the bread crumbs in
   the butter, stirring until they're golden brown.

farro burger

‖‖‖

1 pound farro (also sold as emmer)

Kosher salt

4 ribs celery

1 medium carrot, peeled

½ medium yellow onion

3 cloves garlic

2 to 3 tablespoons canola oil

20 shiitake mushrooms, stems discarded, cut into julienne strips

1 cup vegetarian Worcestershire sauce

6 egg yolks

1 cup shaved parmesan cheese

3 cups panko

Freshly ground pepper

6 burger buns, split and toasted

Handful of dressed assorted greens, for garnish

Makes 6 burgers

I believe in feeding vegetarians food that's as satisfying to them as meat is to omnivores. We use vegetarian Worcestershire sauce, and we use a ton of it. We sauté our mushrooms, deglaze them in the Worcestershire, then combine them with bread crumbs. The other base of our burger is farro, an ancient grain with a full-bodied taste. (You can find it in the bulk bins of natural food stores, though some markets are now stocking it too.) The final patty is like a cross between a sloppy joe and a burger—almost like a risotto cake, but not as dense. It's deliciously meaty, whether you like meat or not.

1. Spread out the farro in a large skillet. Over medium heat, toast the farro for about 5 minutes, shaking the pan to make sure the grains don't burn. You'll know it's done when you hear it crackling and when the grains smell nutty.

2. Bring a large pot of water to a boil. Add the farro and reduce the heat to a simmer; cook until the farro expands and pops, 30 to 45 minutes. It will still be chewy when it's done, so be sure not to overcook it. Drain it in a colander, season to taste with salt, and set aside.

3. Start a mirepoix by dicing the celery, carrot, onion, and garlic into small, even pieces. In a sauté pan over medium-low heat, add the canola oil and cook the vegetables until they are soft but not browned, about 5 to 7 minutes. Transfer the vegetables to a bowl and allow them to cool.

4. Meanwhile, in the same pan, sauté the shiitakes over medium heat for about 5 minutes, or until they release all their water and start to brown. Pour off any excess oil and water from the pan (leaving the mushrooms) and deglaze it with the Worcestershire sauce, pouring the sauce into the pan and stirring and scraping off the browned bits at the bottom with a wooden spoon. Continue cooking the sauce until it has thickened and reduced to a glaze, and is coating the shiitakes in a glaze, about 3 minutes. Remove the pan from the heat.

5. In a large bowl, combine the farro, mirepoix, shiitakes, egg yolks, parmesan, and panko, and mix well. Season to taste with pepper and more salt. Form the mixture into 6 patties. Preheat an outdoor grill or stovetop grill pan on medium. When the grill is hot, brown the patties 2 to 3 minutes on each side, until warmed through. It's OK to make the patties in advance and refrigerate them; if you do this, sear the chilled patties on both sides on the grill or in the grill pan, then transfer the burgers to an ovenproof pan (or leave them in the grill pan) and place in an oven preheated to 350 degrees F for a few minutes to warm them through. Serve the burgers on the toasted buns with the dressed greens and any condiments you like.

sockeye with mashed potatoes

Makes 4 servings

Salmon is an important fish here in the Northwest, and my biggest pet peeve is when it's overcooked. It's so important to treat it with respect and show off the fish the best we can—which means not obliterating it. We cook salmon about three-quarters of the way on one side, then flip it for one minute on the other side, thus ensuring it will be cooked to medium. Do me a favor and try this method. If you are paranoid that it'll undercook your fish, use a digital thermometer. Take the fish off the heat when it reaches 135 degrees F, then let it rest for five minutes before serving. It should be perfect. We use wild sockeye salmon because locally caught ones are more readily available and more affordable here than alternatives like king salmon.

1. Preheat oven to 350 degrees F. Set one stick of butter out at room temperature to soften.

2. In a large roasting pan, generously coat the potatoes in the ¼ cup olive oil and season to taste with salt

1 pound fingerling potatoes, cut to even-size pieces

¼ cup olive oil, plus 2 to 3 tablespoons extra for searing the salmon

Salt and freshly ground pepper

½ cup Crème Fraîche (page 26)

1 cup (2 sticks) butter, divided

1 cup fish stock

½ pound pea vines, cut into 3-inch segments (available at farmers' markets and Asian grocery stores)

½ cup golden beets cooked until fork-tender and cut into ¼-inch dice

2 tablespoons chopped fresh dill

1 cup cherry tomatoes (we like the Sweet 100 variety)

continued

1 tablespoon freshly
squeezed lemon juice

1½ pounds skin-on sockeye
salmon filets, no thicker than
1 inch, cut into 4 pieces

and pepper. Roast them for about 30 minutes, or
until they're fork-tender. Transfer them to a medium
bowl and mash them with a fork—but don't mash too
much. You want large lumps. Gently mix in the crème
fraîche, ½ cup butter, and more salt and pepper to
taste. Set aside in a warm place.

3. In a medium saucepan over medium-high heat,
melt the remaining ½ cup butter and heat until it
is bubbling, making sure it doesn't brown. Add the
fish stock, pea vines, beets, dill, and tomatoes to the
pan. Pour the lemon juice over all. Swirl the pan so
the lemon and butter broth comes together. Keep the
broth warm over low heat.

4. In a medium sauté pan, heat 1 tablespoon olive oil
over medium-high heat. With a paper towel, blot the
skin dry on each piece of salmon and season both
sides to taste with salt and pepper. If your pan is large
enough to cook all four pieces without crowding them,
do so, but it's more likely you'll need to cook them two
at a time. Reduce the heat to medium and gently sear
the salmon, skin side down, for 4 to 5 minutes, or
until you see just a small area that is still raw in the
middle. Flip the salmon with a spatula and remove

the pan from the stove, letting the residual heat cook the remainder of the fish for a minute or two, until it flakes easily with a fork. Repeat with the remaining salmon pieces, adding more olive oil as needed.

5. To serve, place a small pile of mashed potatoes on each plate, making a slight indentation in the top with the back of a spoon. Put a bit of the veggie-broth mix in the indentation, letting some run off the top onto the rest of the potatoes. Top the veggies with a piece of salmon and drizzle a little more broth over the salmon and around the plate.

dessert

Bittersweet Chocolate
"Pie in a Bowl"

Mexican-Style
Hot Chocolate

Chocolate Cake
with Roasted Cherries

Rhubarb-Apple Crisp

Shortbread
and Lemon Curd

Nutella Crostini

DESSERTS WEREN'T a huge part of my world as a chef; I never did a lot of pastry work. So I tend to err on the side of comfort when it comes to the end of a meal: crisps, shortbreads, parfaits—stuff that's easy to put together. That works well on the trailer too. I love desserts, but it's definitely one of those areas where we're not super technical. It gets as simple as memories from my childhood.

I remember when I was younger, one of my mom's "rock star" desserts was apple crisp. She had the perfect balance of the buttery, salty oatmeal crust with tart Granny Smith apples. She would make one pan for the family and one just for me. Along with that she always made fresh whipped cream. That was something she never compromised on—there was always a little Tupperware container with whipped cream in it for the crisp. To this day, I have very particular opinions on crisps; the crust has to be just right, with the perfect sweetness, saltiness, butteriness, and texture.

All in all, I like simple desserts or riffs on them. Shortbread with crème fraîche and lemon curd reminds me of lemon meringue pie. Chocolate pudding with crust pieces, sea salt, and toasted walnuts is about as fancy as I like to get.

bittersweet chocolate "pie in a bowl"

FOR THE PUDDING:

1¾ cups whole milk

½ cup plus 2 tablespoons heavy cream

3 large eggs, slightly beaten

¼ cup cornstarch

¾ cup sugar

3 tablespoons unsweetened cocoa powder

¼ teaspoon salt

2½ ounces dark chocolate (preferably 70 percent cacao, but at least 61 percent), finely chopped

FOR THE CRUST:

4 cups all-purpose flour, plus extra to roll out the dough

¾ cup sugar

1 tablespoon salt

Makes 6 servings

My mom started doing this thing when we were younger called Pie in a Bowl. She would make chocolate pudding, keep it separate in the fridge from the pie crust and whipped cream so it wouldn't get soggy, and build the pie to order. For some reason she and my dad thought it was the coolest idea, and when they knew I was doing a restaurant, they said, "Be sure you use Pie in a Bowl!" We use Theo Chocolate, a great chocolate from a fair-trade factory in Seattle, which results in an amazing pudding, taking it to a whole different level. And anytime you can put sea salt on chocolate, it just needs to happen. Note: You really do need an instant-read thermometer for this recipe to work reliably.

1. To prepare the pudding, heat the milk and cream over medium heat in a metal bowl set over a saucepan of water (the bottom of the bowl shouldn't touch the water) to just below boiling, about 5 to 10 minutes depending on your stove, then reduce the heat to low.

2. In a large bowl, whisk the eggs, cornstarch, sugar, cocoa powder, salt, and chopped chocolate. Carefully drizzle a few tablespoons of the hot milk mixture into the chocolate mixture, whisking constantly. Continue to slowly add the rest of the milk mixture, a bit at a time, whisking as you go. This tempers the eggs so they're not cooked by the hot liquid.

3. Pour the pudding into a large saucepan and cook over medium-high heat, stirring slowly but continually until it reaches 208 degrees F when measured with an instant-read thermometer. Buzz it with an immersion blender or mix with a wooden spoon for about 5 minutes, or until ribbons of beautiful chocoliciousness fall from the spoon when you lift it. You want to see smooth ribbons of pudding, not lumps. Cover the surface of the pudding in the bowl with plastic wrap and refrigerate for 2 to 3 hours, and up to a week.

4. To prepare the crust, preheat the oven to 350 degrees F. Grease a baking sheet with butter and set it aside.

5. Sift the flour, sugar, and salt into a large bowl. Cut the butter into the flour mixture, either using a pastry cutter or rubbing it gently between your fingers, until it has the texture of coarse meal. In a small

1 cup (2 sticks) plus 2 tablespoons butter, chilled and diced (freezing it and grating it works too), plus extra for greasing the baking sheet

2 large eggs, lightly beaten

Splash of whole milk

Pinch or 2 of sea salt

Handful of walnuts or hazelnuts, toasted (optional)

bowl, lightly whisk the eggs and milk. Pour the egg mixture into the flour mixture and stir gently until just incorporated. Wrap the dough in plastic wrap and refrigerate for an hour.

6. Remove the dough from the refrigerator and let it warm at room temperature for a few minutes to facilitate rolling. On a floured surface, roll it out with a rolling pin until it's about ⅛ inch thick. Transfer the dough to the prepared baking sheet—it's OK if it doesn't make the transfer in one piece. Bake for approximately 20 minutes, or until the dough is golden brown. Let it cool slightly, then break it into shards.

7. To serve, spoon a bit of the pudding into each serving bowl, about ½ cup, and tuck a few pieces of pastry around it. Sprinkle a few grains of sea salt on top and scatter with toasted nuts.

mexican-style hot chocolate

Makes five 8-ounce servings

Knowing how to make hot chocolate from scratch is a kitchen basic; it's just as important as knowing how to make a good soup or roast chicken. Hot chocolate has always been a big hit for us on the street, when people want a sugar fix or a sweet warm treat in the cold Seattle winters. This version has a smoky zing.

6 ounces bittersweet or dark chocolate (preferably 70 percent cacao), finely chopped

5 cups whole milk

3 tablespoons sugar

Pinch of salt

1 teaspoon crushed red pepper flakes

1 teaspoon chile powder

5 cinnamon sticks, for garnish

1. In a large saucepan over medium heat, combine the chocolate, milk, sugar, salt, red pepper flakes, and chile powder. Heat the mixture to just below scalding, taking care not to scorch it, then turn the heat off and allow it to cool slightly. Note: The heat brings out the oils, so the longer it sits, the spicier it'll be. Pour it into serving cups and garnish each with a cinnamon stick.

chocolate cake with roasted cherries

FOR THE CHERRIES:

½ cup water

½ cup sugar

¼ cup fresh basil leaves, cut into thin ribbons (chiffonade)

2½ cups pitted cherries

FOR THE CAKE:

2 cups water

1 cup unsweetened cocoa powder

2¾ cups all-purpose flour

2 teaspoons baking soda

½ teaspoon baking powder

½ teaspoon salt

1 cup (2 sticks) butter, softened

2¼ cups sugar

4 large eggs

1½ teaspoons vanilla extract

Makes one 9-inch cake

There are few combinations more delicious than cherries with chocolate. One of the few improvements you can make, though, is to roast the cherries to intensify their goodness. This recipe is something of a cake version of an ice cream sundae: layers of moist, dense chocolate cake topped with whipped cream and cherries. Homemade whipped cream is the only way to eat whipped cream. Ours is light and fluffy, and doesn't have the added sweetness of the store-bought kind. We prefer to use fresh Bing or Rainier cherries, but thawed frozen cherries will work if need be.

1. To prepare the cherries, start by making a simple syrup. Bring the water to a boil in a small saucepan and add the sugar. Remove the pan from the heat, stir until the sugar has dissolved, and allow the syrup to cool slightly. Preheat the broiler to 450 degrees F. Pour the syrup into a large ovenproof skillet, add the basil and cherries, and toss to coat. Broil for 2 minutes, or until the cherries are slightly blistered.

Remove the cherries from the oven and allow them to cool to room temperature.

2. To prepare the cake, preheat the oven to 350 degrees F. Lightly butter or oil a 9-inch round cake pan. Bring the 2 cups of water to a boil in a small saucepan.

3. In a medium bowl, pour the boiling water over the cocoa powder and whisk until smooth. Let the mixture cool. In a separate medium bowl, sift together the flour, baking soda, baking powder, and salt and set aside.

4. In a large bowl, using a hand mixer or a wooden spoon, cream the butter and sugar together until light and fluffy. Beat in the eggs one at time, then stir in the vanilla. Add the flour mixture alternately with the cocoa mixture and grated chocolate. Spread the batter evenly in the prepared pan.

5. Bake for 25 to 30 minutes, or until a toothpick inserted in the center comes out clean. Allow the cake to cool in pan for about 10 minutes and then run a knife around the sides of the cake and invert it onto a wire rack for cooling.

¼ cup grated dark chocolate (preferably 70 percent cacao)

2 cups heavy cream, chilled

2 tablespoons confectioners' sugar

6. In a medium bowl, whip the cream with a hand mixer or whisk by hand. When it is slightly thickened, add the confectioners' sugar. Continue whipping or whisking until the cream is soft and fluffy and forms soft peaks. When you lift the cream with a whisk, it should cling to the whisk—but just barely.

7. To serve, place a slice of cake on each plate and top with a handful of cherries and a few generous spoons of whipped cream.

rhubarb-apple crisp

Makes 8 to 10 servings

My mom would make apple crisp all the time when I was a kid—lots of it. She would always make a pan for the family and a whole other pan for me, because I would eat it for breakfast, lunch, and dinner. I think the key is the crisp—you could almost eat the oat part on its own. Don't be shy about the fat; it may seem like a lot of butter, but there needs to be an appropriate ratio of oats to fat to get that crisp crunch. At Skillet I've tried to carry forward this visceral memory from childhood, adding rhubarb to Mom's plain apple. It's got such a unique flavor and feels right for the Northwest.

1. Preheat oven to 350 degrees F.

2. To prepare the topping, mix all the ingredients in a medium bowl until the texture is coarse and crumbly. To prepare the filling, in a separate large bowl, mix all the ingredients until the fruit is well coated.

FOR THE TOPPING:

½ cup all-purpose flour

½ cup loosely packed dark brown sugar

1 cup rolled oats

½ cup (1 stick) unsalted butter, cut into small dice

1 tablespoon ground cinnamon

1 teaspoon ground allspice

1 tablespoon salt

FOR THE FILLING:

6 apples, preferably Granny Smiths or Galas, cored and thinly sliced with the skin still on

4 stalks rhubarb, cut into 1-inch pieces

½ cup all-purpose flour

½ cup sugar

1 teaspoon freshly grated lemon zest

3. To assemble the crisp, place the fruit mixture in a large baking pan or cast-iron skillet. Top with the oat mixture, pressing down lightly and evenly. Bake for about 45 minutes, or until the sides of the crisp are bubbling. Serve warm with fresh whipped cream.

shortbread and lemon curd

Makes 8 servings

This recipe is adapted from Tartine, *the cookbook from the amazing San Francisco bakery. My copy is spattered with cooking stains, I use it so often. Tartine's attention to detail is just staggering, and I love their aesthetic. Their recipe for shortbread is spot-on. If you follow it, it works. There's no liquid in the recipe, so when you're first making it, you're like, "How is this going to work?" It feels like it's going to be too dry. It isn't. It ends up being perfect for a super crumbly, gentle shortbread.*

1. Preheat the oven to 340 degrees F.

2. To prepare the shortbread, sift the salt, flour, cornstarch, and ⅓ cup sugar into a large bowl. Quickly work the softened butter into the flour mixture, using your fingers, until it just comes together. If it resists, add 1 to 2 teaspoons of lukewarm water.

3. Transfer the dough to a baking sheet and flatten it into an even rectangle about 1-inch thick. Sprinkle

FOR THE SHORTBREAD:

½ teaspoon salt

1¾ cups plus 2 tablespoons all-purpose flour

½ cup plus 2 tablespoons cornstarch

⅓ cup plus ¼ cup sugar, divided

1 cup (2 sticks) plus 2 table-spoons butter, softened until it's almost the consistency of mayonnaise

FOR THE LEMON CURD:

4 medium lemons

3 large eggs, lightly beaten, plus 1 extra yolk

¾ cup plus 2 scant table-spoons granulated sugar

Pinch of salt

1 cup (2 sticks) butter, chilled and cut into small cubes

continued

1 cup Crème Fraîche (page 26)

1 tablespoon confectioners' sugar

the dough with the remaining ¼ cup sugar. Bake the shortbread for about 20 minutes, or until it's pale golden brown. Allow it to cool on the baking sheet and cut it into 2-by-2-inch squares.

4. To prepare the lemon curd, first zest the lemons, then juice them. You want about 5 ounces (½ cup plus 2 tablespoons) of juice and 1 tablespoon grated zest. Reserving the zest, combine the lemon juice, eggs and yolk, sugar, and salt in a metal bowl set over a saucepan of water (the bottom of the bowl shouldn't touch the water); heat over medium-low until the mixture has the consistency of warm yogurt and reaches 180 degrees F when measured with an instant-read thermometer. For food safety purposes, it's really best to use a thermometer here. Remove the curd from the double boiler and allow it to cool to 140 degrees F, whisking from time to time to release some heat. When the curd has cooled, whisk the butter in a handful of cubes at a time, using a gentle, continuous motion, until all the butter is smoothly blended. Transfer the curd to a shallow pan. Cover the curd with plastic wrap and refrigerate at least an hour and up to a week.

5. To serve, mix the crème fraîche and confectioners' sugar. Place a piece of shortbread on each plate. Add a spoonful of the sweetened crème fraîche and a few spoonfuls, about 2 tablespoons, of lemon curd on the shortbread. Scatter a pinch of lemon zest over each plate.

nutella crostini

||||||||||||||||||||||||||||||||||||||||||||||||||||||||||||||||||||||||||||||||||||||||||||||||||||||||||||||||||||

2 slices crusty bread

2 tablespoons butter, softened

2 tablespoons Nutella or other chocolate hazelnut spread

1 banana, sliced

Makes 1 serving

This dish is Simple with a capital S. When Kelli and I were first dating, we would hang out with some great friends, Jenni and Justin, and make dinner with them. We would make this dessert constantly; it's so simple but so tasty. I think the key is that you butter the bread before you toast it. Nutella on crostini is good, but Nutella on butter-toasted crostini is so much better. The beauty of this dish is that you can switch out the fruit as the seasons change. Bananas always work, but you can use berries in season, switching to stone fruit, apples, pears, et cetera— or just enjoy the Nutella on its own.

1. Preheat an outdoor grill or stovetop grill pan on medium-high. When the grill is hot, butter the bread and toast it to your liking. Spread the Nutella on the bread and top with banana slices. If you have a brûlée torch, it's worth the one extra step to slightly caramelize the bananas before serving.

Culinary School and Knowing Yourself

I studied music in college, not cooking. I graduated from Western Washington University. But I really did that just to get a degree, which was a requirement in our family. I'd worked in restaurants since I was 15, and I decided after college that I was going to the Culinary Institute of America (CIA) and was really going to push myself. I'd never really been the best at anything, and I wanted to prove that if I set my mind to it, I would succeed. And I did.

Before, I'd gotten through school with a B average, but I'd never really studied, just coasted. At the CIA I studied a lot. I excelled and wound up being the valedictorian, the speaker for our class at graduation. I kind of proved to myself at that time that I could be a leader. I could do something. And that was what culinary school did for me. I absolutely loved it, though I don't recommend it for everyone. In fact, I don't really recommend it for most people. It's too expensive for the money you make coming out: you're $50,000 in debt and making $10 an hour.

In other industries you can be marginal and still make a living. After culinary school the number of people who will come out with some kind of financially stable future is probably less than 10 percent. That said, I taught for a year at the Art Institute here in Seattle, and I've hired a lot of graduates from their culinary program.

I think what made my own food well received wasn't just my training, it's because I moved around a lot as a kid. I spent my life watching others and watching what worked, whether it was clothes or food or whatever. You learn to assimilate quickly. I got real good at observing and seeing what people did, not just what they said. How that plays out at Skillet is that I'm hyperfocused on what people have thought of my food and how to improve it, and even more hyperfocused on what others do and do better than myself. I was never too concerned whether our food would be liked or not. I felt confident in who I was as a chef. And my confidence didn't stem from a bunch of family members telling me that my potato salad was the best thing they'd ever tasted and I should open a restaurant. I had fed enough people and

carefully watched enough of their reactions to know how I could feed them well.

Most people come out of culinary school with ideas that they're going to be the next great thing, but they don't realize that their skills aren't at that level. Me, I'm not ever going to be Ferran Adrià, being called the greatest chef in the world, but at least I know who I am and what I do well. You need to know that and to know where that lands you around everyone else. Me, I love to build, I love to create. As I went along, I realized that this probably was going to be my value. I'm talented at cooking, but as far as running a kitchen and that kind of thing, that's not my world.

With Skillet, my strength was in what we were putting on the plate and what our voice was. My weakness was the financial aspect, the systems that are needed for any business. Honestly, I fought those systems in the beginning. I wanted to be antibusiness, in a sense. But that wasn't going to be sustainable, so I got partners who specialized in the things I wasn't good at. My current partner, Greg, has run large businesses. He's a salesperson, a ferocious negotiator, an Excel spreadsheet guru—and he'll do it all with a smile. These are all things that are maddening to me, but necessary. Great ideas are all over the place, and somebody who puts a kitchen in an Airstream trailer is a cute story, but without the stability of proper business tools, it's just a story. I don't want to be that. I want to run a business that will be around for ten, twenty, thirty years. I know who I am and what I can do to make that happen.

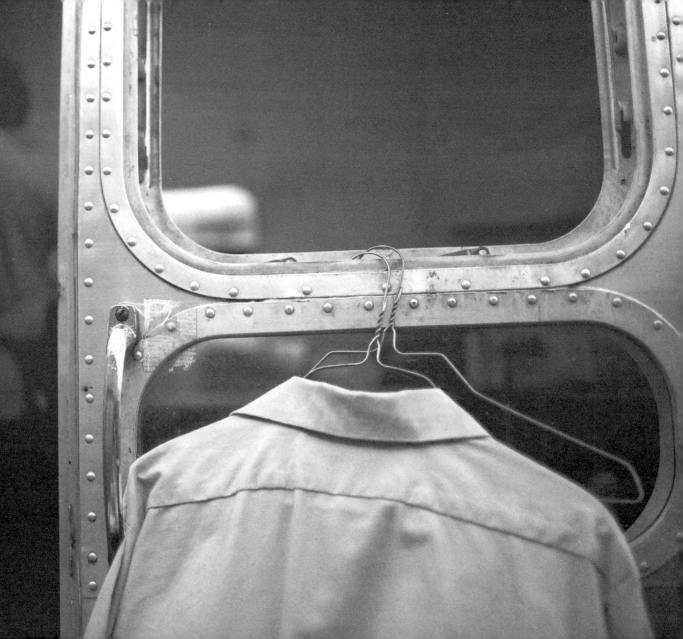

Acknowledgments

Here is a list of people (and a dog) who have supported me. I want to acknowledge them and let them know how appreciative I am of who they are and what role they played and are playing.

First and foremost, I would like to thank my wife, Kelli. Throughout the whole journey of Skillet she has been by my side. She has put as much time and effort in the background as I could have ever asked. I am so incredibly appreciative of her support and love for me; throughout this journey, she has been steadfast, kind, loving, and incredibly supportive in the face of adversity. And on top of that, she has given birth to our beautiful, amazing, and fantastically handsome boys: Huxley George and Wallace James Henderson.

My black lab, Lucca, has been by my side with her gimpy leg and unwavering love . . . she has traveled with me through all the myriad jobs that I have tried along the way to Skillet. She is a part of me.

The original Skillet Diner staff

My mom and dad have been my biggest cheerleaders and fans. I love the fact that they love what I do and are so proud. I can't wait to be able to buy them a house in Cannon Beach someday . . . it will happen, I promise.

Gregory Petrillo, my business partner and the CFO of the Skillet group of companies, has been a massively integral part of Skillet's success. He will be the one at the helm in chapter two of Skillet's journey and our financial success could not be in better hands.

Brian O'Connor has been an incredible partner in the kitchen and a great sounding board. He is an amazing chef, amazing teacher, amazing leader, and has integrity beyond measure. On top of all of that, he is responsible for a ton of recipes in this book . . . thanks, homie.

Skillet Diner would not have happened without Matthew Holzemer's tenacity and passion in this project. He is an even keel, kind, very intelligent, and patient person. He has a great eye for what is "cool" and was an amazing ally in the whole process of creating the diner space. I am honored to call him my friend.

Sarah Jurado truly makes pictures . . . she sees things others don't, and captures emotion, feeling, and clarity. I am so honored and humbled that she was the one with the camera not only for the cookbook but also in numerous instances in Skillet's life.

Thanks to Rebekah Denn for being persistent and constantly keeping me on task. Without her this book could not have been written . . . she put a voice to my rambling thoughts.

Whitney Ricketts dreamed up this crazy idea of a cookbook, and I am so fortunate that she was with me through most of the process. I love the memories of doing crazy events with her and Hebb, cooking on the street or in warehouses. I love her spirit; she is a renegade, and I love it and I love her.

I also want to acknowledge, thank, and generally give a shout out to the following people as well for their influence, effort, time, passion, love, commitment, and overall time spent in the Skillet world . . . Skillet is what it is because of what you have brought to this.

Justin Geel, Parker Eberhard, Robert Pennington, Robin Ludington, Kim Trac, Molly Ringe, Samuel Castrale, Syd Suntha, Brian Chandler, Kat Beck, Matt Solimano, Jon Devaney, Garrett George, Joe Gavin, Noah Cooley, Bob Bosch, Jill Lewallen, Greg Prindle, Alex Prindle, Carl Petrillo, Linda Petrillo, Crellin Pauling, Angela Sommantico, Elliot Tillman, Sammy Benno, Damiana Merryweather, Steven Betts, Thais Oliveira, Elise Moreno, Eliza Simoneau, Matthew Parker, Rick Story, Liz Moody, Robert Haskell, Michael Hebb, Zach Hagen, Jordan Enderle, Josh Batway, Natalie March, Lauren Kile, Rachel Sharpe, Jesse Martinez, Salvador Rojas, Joe Rather, Jono Collins, Adam Trujillo, Jason Patel, Francisco Galeana, Robert Killam, George Chadwick, Julio Robles, Reuben Sanchez, Daniel Garcia, Diego Galeana, Seth Richardson, Brian Klure, Rachel Hall, David Cook, Trevor Green, Patrick Chang, Anthony Smith, Edgar Garcia, Venancio Jiminez, Misael Ornelas, Ricardo Valdivia

Index

About the Author

JOSH HENDERSON has been around the world and then some. Beginning life as a missionary's kid living in Hong Kong and India, he began a circuitous route to becoming a chef. After graduating from Western Washington University with a degree in music, he attended the Culinary Institute of America in Hyde Park, NY. He went on to work for numerous hotels and restaurants over the next ten years.

In 2007, Henderson created Skillet Street Food in Seattle, one of the first food experiences of the street-food movement that has swept the country. Out of a vintage Airstream trailer, he created innovative lunch menus based on American-inspired food prepared with classic technique and seasonal ingredients. The reception from Seattleites was immediate and passionate. In 2011, Skillet opened a brick-and-mortar restaurant in Seattle's Capitol Hill neighborhood. Skillet has been featured in *Real Simple*, *GQ*, *Washington Post*, *Details*, *Sunset*, *Food & Wine*, and on *The Today Show* and The Food Network.

About the Photographer

Seattle-based photographer **SARAH JURADO** began working with Joshua Henderson in 2010 as a part of her collaborative dinner/art series The New Guard. Her photos have been featured in the *New York Times*, *Sunset*, *SPIN*, *The Stranger*, and *Seattle Weekly*. She is 100 percent hooked on Skillet's Kale Caesar Salad.